THE NORTH IRELAND PEACE PROCESS TODAY: ATTEMPTING TO DEAL WITH THE PAST

JOINT MEETING AND HEARING

BEFORE THE

SUBCOMMITTEE ON AFRICA, GLOBAL HEALTH, GLOBAL HUMAN RIGHTS, AND INTERNATIONAL ORGANIZATIONS

AND THE

SUBCOMMITTEE ON EUROPE, EURASIA, AND EMERGING THREATS

OF THE

COMMITTEE ON FOREIGN AFFAIRS HOUSE OF REPRESENTATIVES

ONE HUNDRED THIRTEENTH CONGRESS

SECOND SESSION

MARCH 11, 2014

Serial No. 113–179

Printed for the use of the Committee on Foreign Affairs

Available via the World Wide Web: http://www.foreignaffairs.house.gov/ or http://www.gpo.gov/fdsys/

U.S. GOVERNMENT PRINTING OFFICE

87–142PDF   WASHINGTON : 2014

For sale by the Superintendent of Documents, U.S. Government Printing Office
Internet: bookstore.gpo.gov   Phone: toll free (866) 512–1800; DC area (202) 512–1800
Fax: (202) 512–2104   Mail: Stop IDCC, Washington, DC 20402–0001

COMMITTEE ON FOREIGN AFFAIRS

EDWARD R. ROYCE, California, *Chairman*

CHRISTOPHER H. SMITH, New Jersey
ILEANA ROS-LEHTINEN, Florida
DANA ROHRABACHER, California
STEVE CHABOT, Ohio
JOE WILSON, South Carolina
MICHAEL T. McCAUL, Texas
TED POE, Texas
MATT SALMON, Arizona
TOM MARINO, Pennsylvania
JEFF DUNCAN, South Carolina
ADAM KINZINGER, Illinois
MO BROOKS, Alabama
TOM COTTON, Arkansas
PAUL COOK, California
GEORGE HOLDING, North Carolina
RANDY K. WEBER SR., Texas
SCOTT PERRY, Pennsylvania
STEVE STOCKMAN, Texas
RON DeSANTIS, Florida
DOUG COLLINS, Georgia
MARK MEADOWS, North Carolina
TED S. YOHO, Florida
LUKE MESSER, Indiana

ELIOT L. ENGEL, New York
ENI F.H. FALEOMAVAEGA, American
   Samoa
BRAD SHERMAN, California
GREGORY W. MEEKS, New York
ALBIO SIRES, New Jersey
GERALD E. CONNOLLY, Virginia
THEODORE E. DEUTCH, Florida
BRIAN HIGGINS, New York
KAREN BASS, California
WILLIAM KEATING, Massachusetts
DAVID CICILLINE, Rhode Island
ALAN GRAYSON, Florida
JUAN VARGAS, California
BRADLEY S. SCHNEIDER, Illinois
JOSEPH P. KENNEDY III, Massachusetts
AMI BERA, California
ALAN S. LOWENTHAL, California
GRACE MENG, New York
LOIS FRANKEL, Florida
TULSI GABBARD, Hawaii
JOAQUIN CASTRO, Texas

AMY PORTER, *Chief of Staff*   THOMAS SHEEHY, *Staff Director*

JASON STEINBAUM, *Democratic Staff Director*

(II)

CONTENTS

THE NORTH IRELAND PEACE PROCESS TODAY: ATTEMPTING TO DEAL WITH THE PAST

TUESDAY, MARCH 11, 2014

HOUSE OF REPRESENTATIVES,
SUBCOMMITTEE ON AFRICA, GLOBAL HEALTH,
GLOBAL HUMAN RIGHTS, AND INTERNATIONAL ORGANIZATIONS AND
SUBCOMMITTEE ON EUROPE, EURASIA, AND EMERGING THREATS,
COMMITTEE ON FOREIGN AFFAIRS,
Washington, DC.

The committees met, pursuant to notice, at 2:05 p.m. in room 2172, Rayburn House Office Building, Hon. Christopher H. Smith (chairman of the Subcommittee on Africa, Global Health, Global Human Rights, and International Organizations) presiding.

Mr. SMITH. The hearing of the subcommittees will come to order.

Good afternoon to everybody. I want to welcome everyone and thank them for joining us this afternoon, particularly to our many friends who are testifying today and to others whom I see throughout this room who have been dogged in their determination to bring peace and justice and reconciliation to Northern Ireland.

Today we will inquire into the Northern Ireland peace process, particularly the aspect of it which is called "dealing with the past." Sadly, much of what we will hear about amounts to failures to deal with the past, as in the rejection of the recent proposal by Dr. Richard Haass. Hopefully, that will turn around, but it is at this point not agreed to.

Dr. Haass serves as chair of the Panel of Parties in the Northern Ireland Executive; that is, he was asked to assist in brokering an agreement to move the peace process forward. In that capacity, Dr. Haass spent months consulting and formulating a proposal. In the end, the proposal was not accepted by all of the parties, though it clarified where progress can be made and where sticking points remain, and it is a blueprint for the future.

One of the most important questions that Dr. Haass and the parties dealt with is what will be done with the Historical Inquiries Team and the Police Ombudsman of Northern Island, two key bodies established by the Good Friday Agreement to investigate unsolved murders.

We will discuss Dr. Haass's proposal to replace the HET and the PONI with an Historical Investigations Unit and Baroness O'Loan's suggestion to replace them with a rather different investigative commission—it parallels, but there may be some differences—during this hearing.

For now, I want to underline this: Both agree that the status quo of dealing with The Troubles and the crimes that were committed should be replaced. Likewise, the parties in the Northern Ireland Executive reportedly agreed with this aspect of Dr. Haass's proposal. So the agreement is broad on this point. It is time to move to a better system.

As Dr. Haass's proposal states, "The multiplicity of institutions and vehicles for justice and respect of conflict-related incidents, however, creates confusion and places enormous burdens on the police." The facts alone tell the story of the more than 3,000 Troubles related deaths that occurred between 1968 and 1998. The HET has yet to review some 600 cases involving 800 deaths.

Dr. Haass's proposed Historical Investigations Unit has much to say for it by establishing a single unit with full investigative power to eliminate the overlaps, the contradictions, and waste of resources and the mandates of the two other entities.

Likewise the suggestion of Baroness O'Loan, who served very successfully as police ombudsman from 2000 to 2007 and on several occasions actually came here and testified very bravely. While her idea for an investigative commission that will be "totally independent, fully empowered and fully resourced body . . . with a remit to examine any Troubles-related cases involving death up to 2006 . . ." Lady O'Loan's proposal emphasizes the need for the unimpeachabality of independent agency in order to win the trust of both communities.

In any case, Dr. Haass's proposal remains extremely important on all points. Those involved most closely in the peace process have expressed their confidence that it accurately reflects the current divisions and positions of the parties and will likely serve as an important basis for future discussions.

I think that those who think everything is done and finished, you can close the page on Northern Ireland, really don't know the situation on the ground. That is why we are having this hearing today, and that is why I think these important recommendations need to be taken very seriously all over the world, including in the United States.

We will also hear today about the Finucane case and the British Military Reaction Force. These aspects of dealing with the past were not covered by Dr. Haass's proposal to the Northern Ireland political parties because they deal with matters that are the responsibility of the British Government.

First, the British Government's failure to conduct the promised inquiry into collusion in the 1989 murder of Patrick Finucane remains an open sore.

The British Government has a solemn obligation to initiate a full, independent, public, judicial inquiry that was agreed to as part of the overall peace settlement in Northern Ireland during the Weston Park negotiations.

This obligation, which was undertaken by both governments as part of the Belfast Agreement, one of the outstanding diplomatic achievements of recent decades, was an extremely serious undertaking. In order for the peace process to move forward, the British Government must honor it.

While Prime Minister Cameron has admitted to ''shocking'' levels of collusion between the state and loyalist paramilitaries in the murder of Patrick Finucane and apologized to the Finucane family for it, this does not substitute for a full exposition of the facts behind the British State's involvement in the murder. Rather, the steady increase in the amount of evidence being revealed publicly that the British State colluded with the killers has made honoring that commitment more important than ever.

The British Government committed to implement the recommendation of a judge of international standing on six inquiry cases in 2004. Judge Peter Cory, who we have had at two of my hearings in the past, a very eminent former justice of the Supreme Court in Canada, recommended a public inquiry into the case of Patrick Finucane.

Today, it remains the only case investigated where the recommendation has not been honored, a situation that is deeply unsatisfactory for many reasons, not the least of which it is evidently the one that the British Government is most culpable.

Conversely, it is also the case in which, until the Prime Minister's announcement in December 2012, there has been the greatest level of sustained official denial by various state agencies.

The many previous denials and time that has passed has drained public confidence in parts of the peace process and diminished respect for the rule of law in Northern Ireland.

It must be said that there are those who oppose the peace process and their opposition is dangerous. The failure to address the case of Finucane in the manner proposed by the British Government provides a readily available propaganda tool for those to further their own ends.

Secondly, there is the matter of killings committed by the British Army's Military Reaction Force. From approximately 1971 to 1973, the British Army ran an undercover unit of approximately 40 soldiers who operated out of uniform and in unmarked cars mostly around Belfast.

On November 21, 2013, the BBC program Panorama aired a documentary in which former members of the MRF broke silence on aspects of the unit's operations, confirming what many had suspected for a long time.

The BBC reported that, ''We have investigated the unit and discovered evidence that this branch of the British State sometimes . . . shot unarmed civilians.''

The BBC spoke to seven former members of the MRF and, though the men were careful not to incriminate themselves or each other in specific killings, they made plain that, as the Independent fairly characterized the report—and I quote—''The unit . . . would carry out drive-by shootings against unarmed people on the street without any independent evidence that they were part of the IRA.'' As one of the former members admitted to the BBC, ''We were not there to act like an Army unit—we were there to act like a terror group.''

Now the onus is on the British Government to investigate and punish these crimes. The British Ministry of Defense has said that it has referred the matter to the police for investigation. Unfortunately, the BBC reported that, ''these soldiers were undercover, and what they did has been airbrushed from the official record.''

I would like to now turn to my friend and colleague, Mr. Keating, for any opening comment he might have.

Mr. KEATING. Thank you, Mr. Chairman, for holding this hearing.

It is an honor to welcome Dr. Haass today.

It has been more than 15 years since the Good Friday Agreement. In that time, courage, conviction, and hard work have led to a more peaceful and more prosperous Northern Ireland.

Of course, there is still much work to do. There is still too much tension and mistrust between Catholic and Protestant communities.

No one can dispute the importance of justice for victims of repression and their loved ones, nor can we discount the role that tradition plays in shaping one's identity.

As a former prosecutor, I understand the importance of truth and justice in any criminal investigation, especially one involving allegations of collusion.

Bringing the facts of a case to light and holding perpetrators accountable is an essential part of closure and can pave the way for reconciliation. It is also essential that investigations be independent and free of political influence.

I look forward to hearing from Dr. Haass about his proposal to establish a Historical Investigations Unit. I look forward to hearing from our witnesses on the second panel about their personal experiences.

Despite tremendous personal risk, they have courageously thought to bring to light the facts surrounding political violence in Northern Ireland, violence which impacted each of them profoundly and tragically.

As we examine the importance of dealing with the past, I hope we will also discuss the importance of looking to the future.

In doing so, we should look for the example of those who set aside division and discord in favor of cooperation and compromise. What these men and women have in common is their commitment to building a brighter future as well as their faith in the rule of law and in equality of opportunity.

In that same spirit, I believe one area in particular merits very close scrutiny. Addressing the issue of segregation in both schools and housing is essential to future progress.

Like the champions of segregation in America's not-so-distant past, many in Northern Ireland today argue that segregation is essential to maintaining peace and order. However, our own history shows that segregation only serves to feed fear and resentment. It reinforces stereotypes and it perpetuates inequality.

The United States played a key role in brokering the Good Friday Agreement. We have a responsibility to continue to help the process move forward.

I am concerned that, in the rush to balance the budget, some Members of Congress have acted too hastily in pressing the administration to cut funding for the International Fund for Ireland and the Mitchell Scholarship funding as well.

These programs have been at the forefront of efforts to confront segregation and to promote reconciliation in Northern Ireland. Zeroing out U.S. funding sends exactly the wrong message at a pivotal moment in the Northern Ireland peace process.

With that, I yield back, Mr. Chairman.

Mr. SMITH. Thank you very much, Mr. Keating.

Like to yield to my good friend and colleague, the chairman of Europe, Eurasia, and Emerging Threats Subcommittee, Dana Rohrabacher.

Mr. ROHRABACHER. Well, after hearing the opening statements from my colleagues, it is clear that they know much more about this than I do. And so I will be listening intently and expanding my level of understanding of the facts of what has been going on.

I do know American history, however, and I do know that the bloodiest war that we ever had was with each other. And I don't think we should ever forget that.

And, in fact, at the end of that war, we had President Lincoln, who was inaugurated here at the Capitol for his second inauguration, and he used the famous phrase, ''With malice toward none, with charity for all.''

Unfortunately, one of those attending his second inaugural was John Wilkes Booth. There is a picture of him watching Lincoln being sworn in.

My reading of American history is that it was our insistence of justice being done that created about 100 years of animosity between the North and the South. Had both of our sides decided that they would join each other in remorse over such a slaughter of innocent lives and of fellow Americans, perhaps that would have been different.

And so, as we listen to what is going on in Ireland today, I am hoping that we hear ''With malice toward none and charity for all'' rather than ''Let's find out who did what to whom and punish them now for what they did 10 or 20 years ago, and we are not going to make peace until that happens.'' I hope that is not what I am going to hear.

But I am very interested because I realize that all of our hopes are that the people of Ireland, both North and South, would find some accord by now and that the fact that the talks have broken down—and, again, I am not an expert on this like my colleagues, and I am certainly not an expert on prosecutions as my friend from Massachusetts is and whether or not that is the best road to go to find peace. But it does seem to me if the issue of a flag is significant here or not. And is this the reason that we have this breakdown?

Also, I remember—I worked for the greatest Irish-American President, as you know, and I know there are some Democrats who might disagree with that. But having worked for Ronald Reagan, I actually went to Ireland and advanced his trip to Ireland, and it was one of the great occasions of my life.

I spent a couple weeks there visiting Ballyporeen and all these places where the old Reagans used to go. And I will have to tell you that one of the things that I learned, there were a lot of Protestants there that I met and not one Protestant during that time complained to me that he was being discriminated against in the regular part of Ireland.

So I don't fully understand the psychology of fear that does grip some of the Protestants in Northern Ireland about, perhaps, that there might be some type of persecution going on if there was some sort of unification.

But we cannot just—I don't believe—and I am waiting for the testimony—I don't think that we can move forward with the idea that we are going to right all the wrongs of the past before we reach an agreement for the future, because that just isn't going to happen.

Let's do our best. And I am really interested in seeing if we are doing our best and what suggestions we can have to actually move things along.

Thank you very much, Mr. Chairman.

Mr. SMITH. Thank you, Mr Chairman.

Chair recognizes the gentleman from Texas, Randy Weber.

Mr. WEBER. Thank you, Mr. Chairman.

I am glad to hear that our colleagues are experts. I am looking forward to hearing them and the witnesses. Let's go.

Mr. SMITH. Thank you.

The subcommittees will stand in temporary recess. This is now a briefing portion, pursuant to House rules—it is almost a distinction without a difference—but in order to hear the testimony and the briefing by Baroness Nuala O'Loan.

In 1999, Baroness O'Loan became the first police ombudsman in Northern Ireland and continued in that post until 2007. In that capacity, she was responsible for the investigation of all complaints of criminal behavior and misconduct by police officers and other matters involving possible police wrongdoing, not the subject matter of complaint.

In the course of her work, she has spoken widely at conferences and acted in an advisory capacity to government agencies responsible for policing and police accountability in many countries. In July 2009, she was appointed to the House of Lords and, consequently, to the Peerage in September 2009 as Baroness O'Loan.

Baroness O'Loan has also provided this subcommittee a tremendous amount of input and counsel and wisdom as to what was really happening within the police, all part of her efforts.

She never revealed anything that was not divulgable, but gave us a great sense as to what really was going on behind closed doors and did it as great risk to herself. She had been frequently threatened. She ignored those threats and went on and did an exemplary job as the ombudsman.

So I would like to now welcome, on behalf of the subcommittees, Baroness O'Loan.

STATEMENT OF THE BARONESS NUALA O'LOAN (FORMER POLICE OMBUDSMAN FOR NORTHERN IRELAND)

[The following testimony was delivered via teleconference.]

Baroness O'LOAN. Well, thank you. I am honored to be invited to give testimony here today.

And I would very much like to thank you and to express my gratitude to the people of the United States and to your government for the contribution that you have made over the decades to the peace process, but also to people like me who work at the coalface.

I want to put what we are going to talk about into a little context, if I may. During The Troubles, over 3,600 people died and over 50,000 were injured. Had that happened in the United States, you would have had over ½ million people dead and you would have had over 8 million people injured, and I ask you to consider what the impact of that might have been on your country.

We still have the families of those who died who want to know what happened. We have those seeking justice, and we have those, like the Finucane family, seeking to establish the extent of government responsibility for what happened. Those families come from right across our community.

We have victims of bombings and shootings whose lives have been effectively disabled or limited by their experience, and we have individual investigations of individual bombings or shootings.

But we also have cases like the Omagh bombing or the Ballymurphy killings in 1971, when 11 people were killed over a period of a couple of days by the Parachute Regiment. They included a Catholic priest and a young mother who went to the aid of a young man who had been shot.

We have got Enniskillen; Loughinisland; McGurk's Bar. We have a litany of atrocities. And we still have the families of the people who are seeking the recovery of their loved ones disappeared by the IRA. And we have the highest levels of suicide, mental health problems, and trauma in Europe.

And we only have a piecemeal process, which I think Mr. Haass described well for dealing with the past. So we need a coherent and effective strategy.

If I can just explain what happens at the moment. Four organizations investigate the past. Coroners ask when, where, and how did someone die.

And then the Historic Inquiries Team is part of the police. It is a unit. It doesn't investigate. It just reviews cases. It has no police powers at all. And we know there are difficulties about the way in which it is operated because it had one set of procedures for non-State actors and another set for State actors.

And then we have the PSNI crime investigation department, which carries out the investigations in circumstances in which HET identify investigative opportunities. They investigate anybody who is not a police officer.

And then we have the police ombudsman, who investigates anybody who is a police officer. But, unfortunately, police officers who have been engaged in such crime very often are engaged with others who are not police officers so that we, for example, in an investigation I reported on in 2007, identified collusion between loyalist paramilitaries and the police over a long period from 1991.

So I want to tell you what the defects are in the current system, why it is not working. The first thing is that cases move about between the various organizations and, when they move about, each organization has to start investigating all over again, and that is very costly and very time-consuming.

And then there are strict rules about protecting people so that, as police ombudsman, the people I was investigating would be the police officers. And they would be my suspects and then anybody else would be my witness, be they a soldier, a loyalist paramilitary, a Republican paramilitary, or anybody else, they would be my witness.

For the police, the soldier, the Republican paramilitary, the loyalist paramilitary might well be their suspects, but the police officer couldn't be their suspect. So it is a very complex legal situation.

There are significant problems, as I have said, with the structure and working practices of HET. There is a problem still around access to Special Branch intelligence, and that is critical to investigation.

And is the Legacy Unit, which deals with this, in fact—there are a number of former Special Branch offices there, and I don't think that is calculated to secure trust.

The current arrangements, then, create significant difficulties if you are trying to move toward a prosecution. And I heard Mr. Rohrabacher say that, you know, he didn't want to hear about prosecutions, but the reality is that those who have suffered have the right, in international law, to a proper investigation of their cases.

The Attorney General suggested that Northern Island should simply cease all inquiries, investigations, and inquests into deaths in the past. I think that is superficially attractive because it would allow us to move on, but I don't think you can have a system in which we are prosecuting young men for public order offenses and, if we convict them, then they are criminalized, and, yet, we do not even try to prosecute those who are suspected of murders and bombing and very serious offenses.

It has all recently been complicated by the revelations of what we call the Downey letters, the letters through which some 200 people received letters—letters which—in, certainly, Mr. Downey's case, gave him a situation in which his prosecution was discontinued for the Hyde Park bombing, the deaths of four soldiers and, indeed, of seven horses.

So I think there is a need to build our future on the rule of law. Your poet, Maya Angelou, said that ''History with all its wrenching pain cannot be unlived. If faced with courage, it need not be lived again.'' And I think that is where we have to be.

We all know that, even if we go through prosecution, there may not be—even if we go through investigation, there may not be many prosecutions, but there is a need for the State to act always in accordance with the rule of law.

So I think we do need the kind of independent commission, which Congressman Smith described, to operate in accordance with all national and international standards of investigation.

I think that we need to forthwith terminate the activities of the PSNI and of the police ombudsman in respect to historic deaths, create one single unit which would deal with them.

It would require flexibility and imagination. It would have to be fully empowered in terms of its ability to arrest, search, seize, enter premises, secure scenes, et cetera, et cetera.

Now, there is common purpose, I think, in that I think the people of Northern Ireland have come to the space where it is recognized that we need one unit. Eames-Bradley recommended what was called a Legacy Unit.

That was attractive, but it had a 5-year time limit, which would never have worked. I mean, it took me on one occasion 9 months to find a significant, but very important, witness. So you can't circumscribe it by time.

I think the Haass proposals have moved us a long way. My criticisms of the Haass proposals, with great respect to Dr. Haass, are that, in the language of the Haass statements, it is not stated to be independent and it is not clear what it is a unit of. It is thought in some circles that it will be a unit of the PSNI, and that, I think, would not be independent in the eyes of the people.

It is further suggested that it will report to the Northern Ireland Policing Board. But the problem with that is that the Northern Ireland Policing Board is responsible for the delivery of effective, efficient policing today and it has an interest in the issues which would be under investigation by the Historical Investigations Unit.

There could very well be serving officers in the PSNI today who fall under investigation by the Historic Investigations Unit, and I would see a conflict arising there. And I'm not sure that it could secure the cross-community support.

But I think, if we took the Haass proposal and, if you like, beefed it up to an independent commission, we would be able to bring in some international expertise.

And we have seen a huge contribution by people like George Mitchell, which have really enabled change. So I think a commissioner from outside the UK would be very important.

I have talked about the powers that this organization should have. In reality, everybody knows very few cases will go to prosecution. The decisions to prosecute will be made in the normal way according to the law.

What is important is that ordinary people are able to find out what happened, that as much information as possible is given to them about the circumstances in which their loved one died or in which they themselves were attacked, that that information is provided to them in a respectful way, and that, at the end of the day, we allow—where we can, we set people free of the trauma which is currently limiting so much of our progress, and we allow our country to move on.

So I think that is the essence, perhaps, Congressman Smith, of what I would want to say to you today.

Mr. SMITH. Baroness O'Loan, thank you very much for your very precise and compelling statement.

[The prepared statement of Baroness O'Loan follows:]

SUBMISSION

To: **Committee on Foreign Affairs, US House of Representatives, Washington DC**
Subcommittee on Africa, Global Health, Global Human Rights and International Relations
Subcommittee on Europe, Eurasia and Emerging Threats

From: Baroness Nuala O' Loan DBE MRIA

Date   07.03.2014

NORTHERN IRELAND - DEALING WITH THE PAST

1. Introduction

As a former Police Ombudsman (I established the Office and ran it from 2000 - 2007) and former Irish Special Envoy for Conflict Resolution, working currently in various areas of peace and justice across the world (see attached CV), and as a Member of the House of Lords, I wish to comment primarily on investigation aspects of dealing with the past in Northern Ireland.

In 2010, with Mr. Richard Harvey, a senior British barrister specializing in international human rights, currently working in the Yugoslavia War Crimes Tribunal, I established the Independent Monitoring Panel for the PSNI investigation of Ulster Volunteer Force (UVF) criminality, known as Operation Stafford. Operation Stafford is consequential upon my Police Ombudsman for Northern Ireland (PONI) investigation into a complaint made by Mr. Raymond McCord about the death of his son Raymond Jr. and associated matters, known as Operation Ballast (see www.policeombudsman.org). Mr. Harvey and I were appointed at the behest of both the PSNI and the victims and their families, and have worked closely monitoring the PSNI investigation of many hundreds of UVF crimes, ranging from murders, to attempted murders arson, intimidation, kidnapping, assaults etc.

We have managed to retain the confidence of the families and the police, having access to huge volumes of investigative and intelligence material. This paper also reflects the experiences which we have had in the Independent Monitoring Panel.

I will not comment here on matters such as resources for victims, memorials etc in this submission, though I do have views on these.

2. The current situation with regard to investigation of the past:

Four offices currently deal with the investigation of historic Troubles cases in Northern Ireland:

- HM Coroners (who have a very limited investigative function);

- The Historical Enquiries Team (HET), which is a unit of the PSNI, tasked only to review, but not to investigate, historic cases;

- PSNI C2 (Crime Investigation Dept) which receives historic cases from HET for investigation where there are outstanding investigative opportunities. If PSNI identify any case in which the conduct of a police officer may have resulted in a death, or in a number of other serious cases, the PSNI must refer that matter to PONI for investigation;

- PONI deals with all allegations, current and historic, against members of the PSNI. Where PONI is aware of allegations of criminal behaviour by civilians (non police officers) the Police Ombudsman must refer that matter to the PSNI for investigation.

3. Defects in the current system:

i. The current system results in repeated investigation of the same case by the various investigative arms of the criminal justice system. Cases may come to investigation in a variety of ways:

- HET review;
- Citizen complaint to the PSNI;
- PSNI investigation;
- Citizen complaint to PONI;
- Initiation of investigation by the Police Ombudsman;
- Referral by the Minister for Justice, the Director of Public Prosecutions, a Judge, the Coroner and other possible routes.

ii. Each time one of the investigative bodies embarks on an investigation, it must first review and where necessary re-investigate any previous investigation. This means that there is significant waste of resources as the same tasks are undertaken repeatedly by different organisations.

iii. There are strict rules in relation to investigations which require the protection of the rights of accused persons. If the Police Ombudsman is investigating he must protect the rights of any accused or suspected police officer. He must also treat witnesses, police and non-police, in accordance with the law. A person may be a witness for PONI, and simultaneously a suspect for the PSNI, since only the PSNI can investigate civilians, the military etc. This will inevitably lead to complications as the Police Ombudsman, investigating a case in which a police officer is alleged to have colluded in criminal activity with, for example a paramilitary, cannot take evidence as to that paramilitary's criminal activity, but must instead report it to the PSNI for them to investigate.

iv. Similarly the PSNI will have to treat current and former police officers, under investigation by the Police Ombudsman as witnesses, rather than as suspects, even though they are suspected of wrongdoing. If PSNI becomes aware of grounds to suspect particular types of wrongdoing by police officers they must refer the officers to the Police Ombudsman for investigation.

v. The problems with the structure, remit and some of the working practices of the HET have been documented by HMIC and others.

vi. Access to Special Branch intelligence is subject to gate-keeping by a Legacy Unit which employs former Special Branch officers. This is not calculated to secure the trust of those affected by the arrangements.

vii. The current arrangements create significant difficulties for the PSNI, the HET and the Police Ombudsman when any case is being prepared for submission to the Public Prosecution Service, because of the conflicting remits of the three bodies and their legal responsibilities in matters such as disclosure of information at interview, discovery, handling of evidence, and primacy over witnesses, crime scenes and evidential material.

viii. These difficulties inevitably create significant additional costs and can require significant additional resources and actions by the various units.

ix.. As already indicated, Coroners have limited investigative capacity and a very specific function.

x. There is, in various communities within Northern Ireland, significant distrust of the current systems. During my term as Police Ombudsman, NISRA statistics demonstrated significant faith in the PONI system, despite its lack of powers to investigate soldiers, paramilitaries or civilians. However the ongoing problems and lack of trust in some communities, both loyalist and republican, of the current processes are well evidenced.

xi. For this reason I do not think that retaining the status quo and simply providing a monitoring panel for the HET would address the trust deficiencies which now exist with regard to HET.

Moreover, it is my opinion that the suggestion by the Attorney General, that Northern Ireland should cease all enquiries, investigations and inquests into deaths which preceded the Good Friday agreement, whilst superficially attractive, is not tenable.

The current revelations of "an invisible process" through which some 200 people received letters from the Northern Ireland Office or 10 Downing Street, the contents of which are not currently known, has caused high concern. The letters were revealed when one of them, issued to Mr John Downey, resulted in the collapse of criminal proceedings against him in connection with the 1982 Hyde Park bombings. The explosion killed four soldiers of the Blues & Royals at Hyde Park, Seven of the Blues & Royals' horses also died in the attack. One seriously injured horse, Sefton, survived and was subsequently featured on a number of television programmes and was awarded "Horse of the Year". It is reported that Sefton's rider suffered posttraumatic stress disorder and in 2012 committed suicide after killing his two children. In a second bombing at Regent'sPark seven bandsmen of the Royal Green Jackets died.

The revelation of the existence of these letters and the consequence of one of those letters in the collapse of the Downey case has massive implications for trust in the criminal justice system. There are are currently three Inquiries into the matter : one by a judge, yet to be named and to be appointed by the Prime Minister; one by the Northern Ireland Affairs Committee of the House of Commons, Westminster, and one by the Northern Ireland Policing Board.

The content of each letter, its recipient, and its potential impact on future criminal proceedings has yet to be established.

For our country, emerging from decades of violence there is an obvious need to build our future on sound foundations, which include full compliance with the Rule of Law.

4. A possible solution: An Independent Commission

The American Poet and Writer, Maya Angelou, says that, *'History with all its wrenching pain cannot be unlived. If faced with courage it need not be lived again.'*

The challenge for Northern Ireland is to find a way to deal with the past so as to enable the present and the future. Any solution must be fully compliant with the Rule of Law and all national and international obligations.

I have therefore suggested:

i. The establishment of one totally independent investigative fully empowered and fully resourced body [for these purposes to be called The Investigation Commission, the IC] to operate in accordance with all established national and international standards of investigation), with a remit to examine any Troubles related cases involving death up to 2006, the date of the St. Andrew's Agreement, in which there is a complaint by victims, family members or where there is a reference by Government, by a Judge, by the Coroner, by the Director of Public Prosecutions or any other agreed body such as the Criminal Case Review Commission,or where the IC itself thinks that investigation is necessary in the public interest.

ii. If it transpired that a referral did not fall within the remit of the IC then it would be transferred for investigation in the normal way by either the PSNI or the Police Ombudsman.

iii. The PSNI would cease to investigate any case involving Troubles-related deaths occurring before 2006. The HET would cease to exist. PONI's historic Troubles-related investigations would cease to exist and all the work would be transferred to the new IC. PONI would retain a non-Troubles-related historic investigative capacity so as not to damage confidence in that Office and in policing.

iv. The IC would have to be established in a totally transparent manner, and could be required to be accountable to Parliament in respect of cases which predates the devolution of justice, and to the NI Assembly in respect of cases which may have occurred post devolution.

v. Such a system would require flexibility and imaginative and co-operative working processes between the two legislative bodies, something which exists already in the context of the allocation of control over matters such as the UK's national security interests, international human rights responsibilities, the operation of the CCRC etc.

vi. Accountability, transparency of working procedures and openness would, in any event, be vital to the ability of the IC to attract and maintain public confidence and trust.

The Haass proposal for an Historical Investigations Unit meets some but not all of the requirements which I consider to be fundamental:

i. It is not stated to be independent;

ii.   It is not clear what it is a unit of. It is thought in some circles that it will be a unit of the PSNI;

iii. it suggests that it will report to the Northern Ireland Policing Board (NIPB) but the NIPB is responsible for the delivery of effective efficient policing, and has therefore an interest in the issues, which I consider could constitute a conflict of interests;

iv. the consequence of this is that it is unlikely to secure cross community support which is vital.

vii. **5. Composition of the IC.**

The IC should be headed by at least three Commissioners. Measures must be taken to ensure a sound practical and historical understanding of the complexities of the NI conflict, and a firm grasp of international and national human rights standards for investigating, prosecuting and reporting on violations of fundamental rights.

An international perspective increases the public perception of objectivity. I therefore recommend that one or more of the Commissioners should come from outside the UK.

6. Functions and Powers of the IC

In conducting investigations the IC must operate according to Article 2 ECHR standards for investigation and accountability. Their processes must be effective, as timely as possible, involve families, report back to families etc. It would also require as part of its capacity the ability to engage with perpetrators, and their families.

The IC would require full police powers and privileges, including:

i. Staff vetted in accordance with UK standards, with some personnel vetted to the highest levels to enable access to all systems for intelligence handling, management and storage, and other material etc.

ii. Full powers of arrest, search and seizure;

iii. Full powers to access and seize documentation or property, including all previous Inquiries such as those conducted by Stalker, Sampson, Stevens, Cory, the PSNI and the Police Ombudsman;

iv. Powers to compel witnesses, as in many international investigative systems. This would obviate the current problem of witnesses who refuse to give evidence which would assist an enquiry, even when it in no way implicates them in wrongdoing. The rights of these witnesses would have to be protected in accordance with the law;

v. Powers to access all intelligence and associated data systems;

vi. Powers to secure any incident scene or scenes;

vii. Resources to use all necessary ancillary support e.g. legal, specialist forensic scientists, photography, analysis, medical evidence etc.

viii. An unspecified lifespan. Investigation can be a very protracted process - in one case as Ombudsman it took me nine months to track down one critical witness who had gone out of the jurisdiction. The case Mr. Harvey and I are monitoring has been under active investigation for over three years and the investigative process may continue for at least another two or more years.

ix. Security systems to protect staff, the integrity of investigations, witnesses, buildings etc.

7. Prosecutions, Reports and Recommendations

Prosecutions

i. In reality very few cases would go to prosecution, for a variety of reasons but generally because there would not be a reasonable prospect of conviction (to apply the normal test for prosecution), because of the multiple factors would give rise to a break in the evidential chain etc.

ii. Where prosecutions appear appropriate, however The IC would have the capacity to present cases to the Public Prosecution Service for decision on prosecution.

iii. The decision as to prosecution would be made by the DPP in the normal way.

iv. The matter would then proceed through the courts if so directed by the DPP in the normal way.

v. Sanctions on conviction would be determined by the judge in accordance with the law.

vi. The IC's report on the case would be published after the Prosecution.

Reports

i. Where sufficient grounds for prosecution are not found to exist, in each case the IC would produce and publish a Report on their findings.

ii. The Report should be published in a timely manner, redacted only to the extent necessary to protect life and critical investigative or national security matters. Such redaction should be a capable of challenge before a court.

iii. Matters which are private to the family of the deceased such as details of final moments, messages sent by the deceased to their families etc, would not be for general publication but would be transmitted to the families.

Recommendations

The IC's investigations would inevitably reveal linked crimes and themes such as those I identified in Operation Ballast, and my various investigations as Police Ombudsman. Given what we know thus far, these are virtually certain to reveal collusive activity, significant intelligence handling failings, failures to investigate, and many other problems. All of these should be examined and reported on with a view to ensuring that lessons are learned. Where appropriate the IC should make recommendations.

7.Conclusion

This paper sets out in the briefest possible way one solution to the problem of dealing with unresolved Troubles-related deaths. It provides an opportunity to use tested and established investigative processes which satisfy all the national and international legal requirements on the United Kingdom.

The United Kingdom as a whole, and Northern Ireland in particular, must as constitutional entities, ensure that our future is built upon robust transparent processes which are compliant with the Rule of Law and which complement all that has already been achieved in terms of peace making.

The Baroness O'Loan DBE MRIA

Mr. SMITH. Just very briefly, with regards to the idea of an independent commission, you mention in your written statement that the hope would be that they report to Parliament, as you put it, some of the reporting before 2006, I believe it is, would go to the Parliament and after which it would go to the Northern Ireland Assembly. I might have the date wrong. I am just looking for it.

But to whom in Parliament would it go to? Would it be a special committee? Would it go to the Speaker? The First Minister? How do you see that playing out?

Baroness O'LOAN. Well, I think there are a number of options.

I think it could—because the responsibility, if you like, is a Northern Ireland office responsibility for reserved matters and for the history of Northern Ireland, and that goes to the Home Office and, to some extent, Department of Justice.

There are committees of the Houses of Parliament which are well placed to investigate. For example, I sit on the Joint Committee on Human Rights of the Parliament, which is a joint committee of the House of Commons and the House of Lords, or there is a Northern Ireland Affairs Committee.

But I think reporting to Parliament would take out any suspicion that, you know, there could be cover-up or there could be a failure to be transparent. And that is why I think Parliamentary reporting is the way forward.

Mr. SMITH. You mention that there are conflicts of interest in terms of people who are investigated with the current system that would be eliminated or at least greatly mitigated by an independent commission.

Could you elaborate for the committees those conflicts of interest.

Baroness O'LOAN. Well, as I see it, the Northern Ireland Policing Board, which is an independent organization comprising politicians and independent members, has a responsibility to secure the delivery of effective, efficient policing. It has no powers to conduct investigations or anything like that.

And I think it is for that reason the police ombudsman has to be independent of the Policing Board in order to make independence a reality so that the Policing Board cannot in any way influence what the police ombudsman does.

I think this Historic Investigations Unit or Historic Investigation Commission, whatever it is, has to be in a position in which there can be no suggestion that anybody has influenced in any way any of the decisions which are made within the unit, and I think you will only be able to do that if you take it away from those who have responsibility for policing.

Mr. SMITH. One of your major observations is that access to Special Branch intelligence is subject to gatekeeping by a Legacy Unit which employs former special branch officers. This is not calculated, you go on, to secure the trust of those affected by the arrangements.

How problematic is that? Is that a huge problem?

Baroness O'LOAN. I think it is very problematic. I think it is a big problem.

When I was investigating in the final stages both loyalist and Republican paramilitaries who were alleged to be in collusion with police officers, actually accessing the intelligence was profoundly difficult.

I reported on that issue in my Ballast report, which you will find at the police ombudsman's Web site. And I reported in detail about the difficulties that we had with Special Branch in getting access to the information. You need to have direct access to be able to go in, to open up the computers, to look what is there, and to take it out.

Now, I accept fully that there will have to be proper protection for that information. I accept fully that where agents of the State are involved, there is a need to be conscious of the need to protect their lives and the lives of anybody who maybe affected by their activities. But that doesn't mean it is impossible.

I am very clear that, having done it myself, it can be done and that that access, that direct access to intelligence, should not be the subject of gatekeeping and it certainly shouldn't be the subject of gatekeeping by former Special Branch officers, who may be perfectly good, honest people, but who may be perceived to have, if you like, a motive not to be as honest and transparent as perhaps they would intend to be.

Mr. SMITH. And just two final points.

And one of the main reasons for convening this hearing today is, I think, the mistaken view that somehow matters in Northern Ireland has moved on, that peace has broken out, reconciliation has broken out, but these long-simmering and festering injustices, with collusion being a part of it, remain unresolved.

And I would hope the press and Members of Congress and members of parliaments everywhere would understand that there are festering sores. Justice delayed is justice denied. And in this case we are denying it. Things have not happened that were supposed to happen, one of which is the special public inquiry into Patrick Finucane's assassination.

Geraldine Finucane is here and will be testifying, if you want to speak to that.

But, also, this idea that Northern Ireland is off the radar screen for most people, it ought not to be. And, again, I think Ambassador Haass did a yeoman's work.

And I would recommend—and he says it in his testimony—everyone should read the proposed agreement, December 31st, 2013, and it ought to become a subject of widespread, hopefully, discussion and action. But the page has not been turned. There are still unresolved problems that need to be fixed.

Baroness O'LOAN. I agree with you absolutely. I think that what the politicians and Dr. Haass achieved over that 6 months built very much upon the Eames-Bradley report.

And I think there is a potential for a way of dealing with the past, subject to some of the criticisms I have made, and I think we have to find the courage to go on and to do it.

I am not going to talk about Mrs. Finucane's case. I never investigated it. It was not one which came to me. I think she is the person best placed to articulate the difficulties and the trauma of what that family experienced. So I would simply pay tribute to her and leave it for her.

Mr. SMITH. Thank you.

Mr. Keating.

Mr. KEATING. Thank you very much for your statement. I just have one area I just wanted to get a handle on a little bit more.

And what is the scope? What would be the scope of the independent commission in terms of your view and the number of cases that they would look at, the number of investigations?

Because I think, when you get a better handle—at least, if I get a better handle on the scope, I might have a better view of some of the better ways to form that commission or have it conduct its work.

Baroness O'LOAN. I think it would have to be responsible for the investigation of all deaths resulting from The Troubles. And I think politicians will agree on the cutoff, whether it is 2006 or 2010, when justice was devolved. I don't know.

But it should have the power and the ability to investigate actors of the State, such as agents of the State, soldiers, police officers, and ordinary, if you like, Republican and loyalist paramilitaries, anyone who was engaged in any way in any of the deaths which occurred during The Troubles.

It should have full police powers. It should be as powerful as, for example, your FBI or our Metropolitan Police Service so there should be absolutely no question that it can do what it has to do.

I think probably the most important thing is that it actually has the courage to exercise those powers because, you know, there can be a lot of pressure on people not to.

Mr. KEATING. I was just trying to contemplate if there was any kind of estimate on—maybe Dr. Haass might be helpful, too—on the number of cases.

Because we have a seldom-used process in the U.S. of an inquest, where a judge would sit in a position and have all kinds of powers that you had mentioned and deal with an individual investigation itself and the judge—it wouldn't necessarily lead to a prosecution, but they could issue a report which then would take the next step toward potential legal action.

So I was thinking, could this ever be done or would it be a secondary step to actually have an individual review of incidents themselves?

Baroness O'LOAN. We have had individual reviews, particularly the Cory reports, and Judge Cory did a number of the cases. We have 3,600 deaths, approximately, to answer your question about the specific numbers.

Some of them have been very well investigated and, in respect to those, there will be no further need for investigation. And there is a significant number in respect to which considerable further investigation is required.

I would see no benefit in appointing a judge to do it, although you could have a judicial figure heading your historic unit or your independent commission. The important thing is that whoever does it has the power to do it properly.

And I think it does take a compilation of police powers, investigation powers, judicial powers, legal powers, et cetera, to do that effectively. So we have had judge-led inquiries, and that possibly is what Mrs. Finucane is seeking. But I don't see them as being the answer to everything.

There are calls for what we call Hillsborough-type inquiries. I don't know if you are aware of that. But this was a situation in which a number of—well, I think 128 people died at a football match because of defective policing and an inquiry was led by a judge, but with academic researchers and police officers to investigate it, and produced a report which has now led to a police investigation. So we have a number of models which are available.

My concern is that, if we could clarify to make it simple, if we could have one commission which could actually do everything and if we were prepared to put the money into enabling it to do it, then it could be a system in which people could have confidence and it could begin to draw the line under the past.

Mr. KEATING. Great.

I think, given the number that you mentioned, a commission is better approach initially, because the numbers are much too high.

But maybe, as a secondary approach, that is something that could be—for certain cases, could be developed, something that could be looked at.

Thank you very much.

I yield back.

Mr. SMITH. Thank you, Mr. Keating.

Chairman Rohrabacher.

Mr. ROHRABACHER. Thank you very much.

It just seems to me that what you are talking about—and I am sorry to—you know, just to be very frank, it sounds like you are dwelling so much on the violence of the past that you may not be able to lay the groundwork for a very pleasant future for children today.

I will just have to say that—well, let me ask you how extensive you want this commission to delve into that and what kind of punishment you think should be dealt out to people who were engaged in what at that time was a chaotic situation in which people were losing their lives. There were explosions. There were police brutalities. You had an internal conflict, and some people make wrong decisions in situations like that.

Do you believe that political leaders, people who were in elected office at that time, for example, who oversaw police policy—and we know that the police committed certain acts that are—that we now look back on that were not only not right, but were not legal—you would have those—what would you have those political leaders who turned their backs and just let this happen do?

Are you saying that now we are going to contact people who are 80 and 90 years old and put them before a court and ship them off to prison and, thus, they can fully explain why they let these murderers go who beat some witness to death 30, 40 years ago? What extent do you want—you want to take an 80-year-old man or an 80-year-old woman who was a police commissioner, let's say— is it your idea that we need to take that person to justice, march them out, put them on trial, and put them in prison for what they did or what they didn't do?

Baroness O'LOAN. I think it is most unlikely—the scenario which you describe is most unlikely, in the first instance.

What you need for a prosecution is an unbroken chain of evidence. And we do have law which says that anybody who is convicted of a Troubles related offense can only serve a maximum of 2 years. So that goes to your question about punishment. It is a maximum of 2 years.

But the reality—if I may say, sir, the reality is that there are very likely to be very few of those situations.

I have to say to you again, where—you know, in London, where I am at the moment—in London, for example, the Metropolitan Police are currently conducting an investigation—another investigation into the murder of a young man called Stephen Lawrence who died nearly 30 years ago. We are also having a lot of child abuse investigations. I think you have those, too. Historic ones.

I can't see the difference between—I can't see why a State would choose to investigate things like abuse of children, but choose not to investigate the much greater abuse of children which resulted from murdering their fathers and mothers.

So I think that we have to stand back from the emotion, we have to accept that there will be very few cases. When people get to the age group that you are talking about, they very often can't remember, they may have difficulties such as forms of dementia and things like that. Nobody is going to seek to take those people before the court.

But it is important that there be a process which is compliant with the law. And the law says that, if somebody has died, then the State has an obligation to investigate and to inform the families.

Mr. ROHRABACHER. You know, in my——

Baroness O'LOAN. Try to—if we try——

Mr. ROHRABACHER. In my area in Orange County, I am very much in favor of when the police get out of hand—and there have been several cases of that in the last couple years, where the police have murdered—for example, in Fullerton, California, where the police murdered some poor homeless guy who probably mouthed off to them. And there is no doubt that we need to bring people like that to justice.

But to think about 20 or 30 years from now bringing the person who oversaw the police in city government who then perhaps let these guys go, if that is what happened, that we are going to bring justice to the case now, you will have—you're talking about crimes that exist—that happened 30 years ago; are you not?

Twenty, thirty years ago——

Baroness O'LOAN. But I have——

Mr. ROHRABACHER. And if they are 20, 30 years ago, the people who oversaw that are older people and may or may not have the ability to defend themselves against charges that somebody may—somebody may be holding grudges; somebody may not—it seems to me that what you are talking about is opening up a pandora's box that is a never-ending situation, at least for a century, while—you know, when Communism fell, they didn't take every local police chief who let their police do certain crimes against people and they didn't seek vengeance. And, thus, Communism was allowed to move on, and the people of Eastern Europe have moved on.

It seems to me that what you are talking about is not moving on but, instead, dwelling on these things.

Go right ahead and answer. I am sorry.

Baroness O'LOAN. What you have to understand is that it is not me that is saying this. It is the people who suffered at the hands of those who murdered their loved ones. And Mrs. Finucane will speak to you on this issue very clearly, I am quite sure.

What I would want to say to you is that, again, we are not looking at overseers, for the most part. We are not looking at police commissioners.

We are looking at the situation in which an individual death occurred, and for the most part, it will be paramilitaries who caused those deaths with no police involvement either. So we are looking at all the cases.

It is a limited number, 3,600. In respect to a number of them, there have already been trials. There have already been prosecutions and convictions. So it is the outstanding numbers that we need to look at.

And I think we need to have a process whereby people opt in if they want their case investigated, because there are some families who don't want any further investigation.

The biggest thing the families want—and most families would say to me that they are not interested so much in prosecution. They want to know what happened, how it happened, and why it happened. And that, I think, is the basis upon which you build society.

And I think I said when I presented to you that I do not believe that this would lead to many prosecutions. That has been my experience doing historic cases. But it is profoundly important that you tell people what happened.

Mr. ROHRABACHER. I think that you are well motivated. And, of course, who doesn't condemn the horrible crimes that you are talking about?

There were some horrible crimes that were committed on both sides of this conflict, but the people who were in political power have certain more responsibility than do people who were not in power at the time.

So let me just note that your motives are good, and I commend you for it. I don't believe what you are talking about will lead to a more peaceful situation in that part of the world, and I—but I know that you are talking about justice, which is something we should all be about.

I will just end with this one thing. When I was a young person, one of the first lessons that I learned was that you have got to quit picking at the scab or your wound will never heal. That is the first thing I learned. I would hope that we are not just picking at scabs here. I hope we are looking to heal things.

And I know that you are—you believe that, once all the facts get out, there is going to be a better chance at a national healing among the people of Ireland and Northern Ireland, and I understand that.

And as I say, it is well motivated. I don't know if that is what will be the result, a healing, or just an opening up of a wound.

Thank you very much.

Baroness O'LOAN. I can only speak from experience and tell you that, from the work which I did over the 7 years when I was police ombudsman, trust in the police was lower and the process through which people began to realize that the police were accountable for their actions led to enhanced confidence in policing. Everybody from the chief of police to political leaders acknowledged that fact.

And I think, therefore, there is experience in Northern Ireland which suggests that, if we can find a way of dealing with the past—and I have to tell you, in so many cases, there is no unbro- ken chain of evidence, papers have been destroyed, they have been blown up, et cetera, et cetera. So we can—it will always be a limited process, in so many cases.

But, as I said, I don't think we can have a legal system which criminalizes young people for marching down the street or protesting against those who marched down the street whilst it fails to deal with those who are suspected of more serious crime.

Mr. SMITH. Mr. Weber.

Mr. WEBER. I have no questions.

Mr. SMITH. Chair recognizes Mr. Holding, who I would note parenthetically is the former U.S. Attorney for the Eastern Northern Carolina district.

Mr. HOLDING. Well, thank you, Mr. Chairman.

I really don't have any questions at this time. But I appreciate the informative testimony and listening to the questions of my learned colleagues.

Mr. SMITH. Thank you very much.

Baroness O'Loan, thank you so much for your statement. This is our 15th hearing that we have held on policing or injustices that—especially some of those that have been historical and have remained unresolved.

We take the view on—at least I do—that there is no statute of limitations on murder. As a matter of fact, some of the most important prosecutions, even recently here in the United States, have focused on people who have been murdered during the civil rights movement or, even before the civil rights movement got off the ground here in the United States. I take the view that accountability is the ultimate confidence-builder.

And I take your point, as ombudsman, that there was a rising tide of confidence because of the work that was done, not as a reaction to anything else, but because of the good work that you and others did. And justice is the prerequisite, I think, for a sound and functioning society.

So I do thank you for your exemplary service for so many years.

Mr. Keating.

Mr. KEATING. Thank you, Mr. Chairman.

One other thought I would just like to say. As we look at this, I am struck by a saying of a Nobel Prize recipient we have in the U.S., Elie Wiesel.

I think it comes to the core of what you are looking for, Baroness, and that is the fact that it is clear that hatred was a factor over these many decades.

And I am reminded of his comment that the opposite of hate is not love, but it is indifference. And I think that it is important to look at these issues, it is important that we understand those issues because we can't move forward without that.

So I thank you for your comments.

Mr. SMITH. Thank you, Baroness.

Baroness O'LOAN. Thank you.

[Whereupon, the subcommittees concluded their briefing and moved to the hearing.]

Mr. SMITH. The subcommittees now will resume their hearing.

We will now welcome our first witness for the hearing, Ambassador Richard Haass, former U.S. Special Envoy to Northern Ireland.

Ambassador Haass served as U.S. Special Envoy to Northern Ireland from 2001 to 2003. More recently, 2013, he served as the independent chair of the official multi-party panel established to address some of the most divisive political issues affecting Northern Ireland.

He is currently the president of the Council on Foreign Relations. He has also been the Director of Policy Planning for the U.S. Department of State, was Special Assistant to President George H.W. Bush, and was Senior Director for Near East and South Asian Affairs on the staff of the National Security Council from 1989 to 1983.

Ambassador Haass, the floor is yours.

STATEMENT OF THE HONORABLE RICHARD N. HAASS, CHAIR, PANEL OF PARTIES IN THE NORTHERN IRELAND EXECUTIVE

Ambassador HAASS. Chairman Smith, Chairman Rohrabacher, thank you for this opportunity to discuss the Northern Ireland peace process. What I will do is make some fairly brief opening remarks and ask simply that my full statement be put in the record.

Mr. SMITH. Without objection, so ordered.

Ambassador HAASS. I have twice now been intimately involved with this issue. From 2001 to 2003, I was the U.S. envoy to the Northern Ireland peace process during the presidency of George W. Bush. And as Chairman Smith said, over the last 6 months of last year, I was the chair of the Panel of Parties process in the Northern Ireland Executive.

But there are important differences between the two periods that go beyond whom I was representing. When I represented the Bush administration more than a decade ago, the principal challenge was to implement the recently negotiated Good Friday Agreement, also referred to as the Belfast Agreement of 1998.

And as has been referred to, that agreement constituted a major milestone, because what it did was to effectively bring to an end the violence that had taken over 3,500 lives over 3 decades.

The 1998 agreement and the subsequent efforts, to be sure, advanced the peace process, but in no way did they complete it, nor did they bring about a normal society. This is not simply my judgment. This judgment was and is widely shared.

Indeed, in the spring of 2013, the office of the First Minister and deputy First Minister in Northern Ireland proposed a process that would tackle some of the remaining issues. This process would be one that would involve all five parties of the Northern Ireland Executive and it would require, in their view, an independent chair.

I was then asked by the First Minister and deputy First Minister in July 2013 to be that independent chair. And based in large part on their support of this process, I accepted, after which I asked

Professor Meghan O'Sullivan of Harvard University to be the vice chair.

Now, our remit was to forge a consensus among the participating parties in three areas: The use of flags and emblems both in official spaces and in informal public displays; the regulation of the thousands of parades, commemorations, and protests that take place each year; and contending with the past, the principal subject of today's hearing.

By the end of 2013, we had made seven trips to Northern Ireland, as well as visits to London and Dublin. There were 33 days of meetings, most involving the five parties either separately or collectively.

There were also more than 100 meetings with 500 people, representing a wide range of civil society organizations, along with business, religious, and political representatives.

In addition, we received more than 600 submissions from individuals and groups on a Web site that we established. And the draft agreement that emerged on December 31 of last year is now in the public domain.

And here, too, Mr. Chairman, I ask that it be made part of your record.

Mr. SMITH. Without objection, so ordered.

Ambassador HAASS. The goal of this process was to produce an accord acceptable to all five parties that would also help Northern Ireland address some of the most vexing issues and, in the process, reduce sectarianism and promote reconciliation.

Just to be clear, the text does not always represent my or Professor O'Sullivan's view of what would be optimal. Rather, the December 31 document is and was our best effort to produce a set of carefully balanced compromises that we believed would both meet the various needs of the political parties and leave the society better off. And we reserved at the time the right to issue our own assessments and make recommendations, a step we continue to consider and may indeed well take.

In two areas, in the areas of parades and the past, the text yields extensively and fairly with the challenges Northern Ireland confronts.

In the realm of flags and emblems, however, where no amount of consensus proved possible, the document essentially calls for a follow-on process.

Now, the draft document has the most to offer in the subject of your hearing today, in the area of helping Northern Ireland address its past. The proposed mechanisms would increase the chances that families could learn more about the specific circumstances around and reasons for the death of loved ones.

The agreement—and somewhat different than described by Baroness O'Loan—the agreement would create an independent Historical Investigations Unit with investigative powers that would take the place of both the Historical Enquiries Team, the HET, and the historical role of the existing police ombudsman office.

But this new institution would be created and empowered in a way that in no way would grant the perpetrators of violent acts amnesty. This is an important difference between what was proposed here and what is often proposed in other post-conflict societies because the agreement, as written, would not require that the pursuit of greater information come at the cost of potential prosecution.

And I know Congressman Rohrabacher has some concerns about this, and I will be glad to discuss why I believe this, on balance, was the appropriate way to proceed.

In addition, in order to help make better sense of the past, one entity was to be established that would also assess the presence or existence of certain patterns or themes involving both governments and paramilitaries and report on the degree of cooperation with this process by both.

The text calls for public statements of acknowledgment of responsibility by individuals, organizations, and governments that were involved in the conflict, and I believe such statements are essential if there is to be healing at either the individual or societal level. The text also establishes new mechanisms and procedures to help defuse the tensions around parades, protests, and commemorations.

Now, while a critical component of Northern Ireland's culture and history, these events can also be an obstacle to good relations. The right of free expression must be balanced not only against other rights, but also against the goal of creating a less divided society of 1.8 million people sharing a space the size of the State of Connecticut.

The issue of flags proved the most difficult. Flags are the most visible and emotive, but not the only representation of what many in Northern Ireland hold so dear: Sovereignty, allegiance, identity.

The text calls for public debate across Northern Ireland on such issues as flags, emblems, the role of the Irish language, a bill of rights, and the commission overseeing this debate would then submit a report to the leaders of Northern Ireland with its recommendations.

Our mandate ran until the end of the year, until December 31. This was a deadline established by the Northern Ireland Government, and at that point we ended the talks. Two of the parties, Sinn Fein and the Social and Democratic and Labor Party, the SDLP, endorsed the text in its entirety; a third-party, Alliance, endorsed the part of the text that deals with the past; and the other two parties, the DUP, the Democratic Unionist Party, and the UUP, the Ulster Unionist Party, decided not to endorse the text.

Now, some have interpreted this outcome as an indication that the agreement met more nationalist than unionist concerns. Both Professor O'Sullivan and I reject this categorization. There is a great deal in the proposal for unionists; there is a great deal in the proposed text for nationalists. There is also a great deal in the text for the many in Northern Ireland who are not politically aligned, but who simply want to have a better understanding of the past and more reason to look forward to their future.

To be candid, this outcome was a disappointment. The draft reflects months of conversations with individuals and groups within Northern Ireland as well as the five parties. It reflects the often competing preferences of the five parties and what was required to bridge them.

We understand that no party is fully comfortable with the December 31 text, and that should surprise no one here, indeed no one anywhere. Politics inevitably requires that each party accepts some elements it views as disagreeable in order to advance the greater good.

And here I can do no better than to quote Henry Kissinger, who recently wrote that the test of any proposed accord ''is not absolute satisfaction, but balanced dissatisfaction.'' I believe the December 31 Northern Ireland text met this test and then some.

Leaders must be prepared to take and make this case to their constituents and to the broader public. The true definition of leadership is a willingness to tell your supporters, not just your opponents, what they do not want to hear. A second requirement of leadership is to speak to those across the political divide, to reassure them that their core interests are not threatened, and that what is in the interest of one party or group or tradition need not be inconsistent with that of the other. And in the case of Northern Ireland, there is a third requirement for leaders: As appropriate, to acknowledge responsibility for the past.

Since December 31, the parties have held a number of meetings in an effort to narrow their remaining differences and to add some needed detail, such as in the area of what would constitute a code of conduct for parades and protests. This effort, though, came to something of a halt when it was disclosed that the British Government had sent letters to nearly 200 people, assuring them that they were not wanted by the police. Virtually all I know about these letters is what I have learned from public exchanges over the past few weeks.

It is my understanding that the letters essentially inform recipients that there was insufficient evidence to pursue or prosecute them should they return to the United Kingdom. But it is also my understanding that the letters made clear that prosecution could come about if new information regarding violations of the law came to light. In short, the letters did not offer amnesty, and I know of nothing in their content that would justify anyone walking away from the process we are discussing here today.

So where do things go from here? I agree with the First Minister when he says that the three issues at the center of the talks still need to be dealt with. To this, though, I would add a sense of urgency. The passage of time will not heal Northern Ireland's society. To the contrary, absent political progress, the passage of time will only create an environment in which social division intensifies, violence increases, investment is scared off, alienation grows, and the most talented depart.

Northern Ireland is often cited as a model of peace building, but this is premature. Yes, the society has come a long ways from where it was two decades ago, but it still has a long ways to go before it sets an example others will want to emulate. I hope Northern Ireland's leaders are up to the challenge.

Mr. Chairman, Mr. Congressman, thank you again for this opportunity. I look forward to answering your questions.

[The prepared statement of Mr. Haass follows:]

COUNCIL *on*
FOREIGN
RELATIONS

March 11, 2014

Prepared statement by
Richard N. Haass
President
Council on Foreign Relations
and
Former Independent Chair
Panel of Parties in the Northern Ireland Executive

Before the
Committee on Foreign Affairs
Subcommittee on Africa, Global Health, Global Human Rights, and International
Organizations
and
Subcommittee on Europe, Eurasia, and Emerging Threats
United States House of Representatives
2nd Session, 113th Congress

Hearing on the Northern Ireland Peace Process Today: Attempting to Deal With the Past

Chairman Smith, Chairman Rohrabacher:

I thank you for this opportunity to appear before these two subcommittees of the House Committee on Foreign Affairs to discuss the Northern Ireland peace process.

I have twice been intimately involved with this issue. For three years, from 2001 to 2003, I was the US envoy to the Northern Ireland peace process. And more recently, over the last six months of 2013, I was the chair of the Panel of Parties in the Northern Ireland Executive.

When I represented the Bush Administration in this realm more than a decade ago, the principal challenge was to implement the recently negotiated Good Friday Agreement – also referred to as the Belfast Agreement – of 1998. That agreement constituted a major milestone, effectively bringing to an end the violence that had taken over 3,500 lives and all too often dominated Northern Ireland (and, at times, life in Ireland and the rest of the United Kingdom, as well) for three decades. The challenge facing those of us who came after the agreement was concluded was to bring about the decommissioning of arms still widely held by paramilitary groups and to help stand up local political, policing, and legal institutions.

These efforts advanced the peace process, but in no way did they complete it. Nor did they bring about what might be described as a normal society. This was a widely shared judgment among outsiders and Northern Ireland's politicians alike. Indeed, in the Spring of 2013, the Office of the First Minister and Deputy First Minister published "Together: Building a United Community," a document calling for a large number of initiatives that would, if implemented, help ameliorate many of Northern Ireland's remaining divisions. One specific proposal was to establish a political process that would tackle some of the most divisive issues. The process would involve all five parties of the Northern Ireland Executive and an independent chair.

I was asked by the First Minister and deputy First Minister in July to become the independent chair. Based in large part upon their support for the process, I accepted this position, after which I immediately asked Meghan O'Sullivan, a professor at Harvard's John F. Kennedy School of Government who had previously worked closely with me when I was the US envoy to the Northern Ireland peace process, to be the Vice-Chair. Our remit was to forge a consensus among the participating parties in three areas: the use of flags and emblems, both in official spaces and in informal public displays; the regulation of the thousands of parades, commemorations, and attendant protests that take place each year; and contending with the past. We assembled a small team and got down to work.

By the end of the year, we had made seven trips to Northern Ireland as well as additional trips to London and Dublin. There were 33 days of meetings and negotiations, most involving the five parties either separately or collectively. There were also more than 100 meetings with 500 people representing a wide range of civil society organizations, along with business, religious, and political representatives. We received some 600 submissions from interested individuals and groups on a website (PanelofPartiesNIE.com) that we established.

The draft agreement that emerged from this process on December 31, 2013 is in the public domain, and I very much hope it gets wide readership. The goal was to produce an accord acceptable to all five parties that would help Northern Ireland address some of its most vexing issues and, in the process, reduce sectarianism and promote reconciliation. The text does not always represent my or Professor O'Sullivan's view of what would be optimal for Northern Ireland society now or in the future. Rather, the December 31 document is and was our best effort to produce a set of carefully balanced compromises that we believed would meet the various needs of the political parties and still leave the society as a whole better off. We reserved the right to issue our own assessments and recommendations, a step that we continue to consider and may well take in coming weeks. In two areas – parades and the past – the text deals extensively and I believe fairly with the challenges Northern Ireland confronts. In the realm of flags and emblems, where despite intensive efforts no amount of consensus proved possible, it calls for a follow-on process.

More specifically, the draft agreement has the most to offer in helping Northern Ireland address its difficult past. I attribute this, in large part, to the critical role victims and survivors have played in encouraging new thinking. The agreement places a high priority on the principle of choice – the notion that victims and survivors must be able to choose, wherever possible, how and whether they interact with organizations and processes addressing the past. This principle runs throughout provisions to provide quality services to victims in a sensitive and compassionate manner, and extends to the question of how legal cases are handled.

The proposed mechanisms would increase the chances that families could learn more about the specific circumstances around and reasons for the death of loved ones. But they would do so in a way that does not grant the perpetrators of violent acts amnesty for their actions. Unlike in many other post-conflict societies, the agreement as written would not require that the pursuit of greater information come at the cost of potential prosecution.

The text would establish a new Historical Investigations Unit, with full investigative powers equivalent to those of the Police Service of Northern Ireland, to take over cases being addressed by the already-existing Historical Enquiries Team and the historical unit of the Police Ombudsman for Northern Ireland. The role of this new entity would be to investigate unsolved conflict-related deaths and transfer findings for prosecutions where evidence warranted.

The draft agreement would also create an Independent Commission for Information Retrieval (ICIR) that would enable victims and survivors to seek and privately receive information about conflict-related events separately from the justice system. To encourage people to come forward and cooperate with this undertaking, the agreement would provide limited immunity, i.e., information provided to the ICIR could not be used to prosecute, although nothing would preclude prosecution if grounds for doing so emerged from other sources or by other means. In order to help make better sense of the past, the ICIR would also assess the presence of certain patterns or themes involving governments and paramilitaries and report on the degree of cooperation with this process by both. Last, the text calls for public statements of acknowledgment of responsibility by individuals, organizations, and governments that were involved in the conflict. Such statements are essential if there is to be healing at either the individual or societal levels.

Second, the text seeks to defuse the tension around parades, protests, and certain commemorations. While a critical component of Northern Ireland's culture and history, these events can also be a flashpoint for unrest and an obstacle to good relations. The right of free expression that is part of marching must be balanced not only against other rights but also against the goal of creating a less-divided society of 1.8 million people sharing a space the size of Connecticut.

The agreement seeks to distinguish the overwhelming majority of parades, which pass off peacefully each year, from the small number that are contentious. It offers a new institutional architecture for notifying events and adjudicating disputes, prioritizes local dialogue and mediation, and establishes a more transparent means of decision-making and oversight. It also sets forth some of the principles that would inform a new code of conduct that would be enshrined in law.

The issue of flags proved the most difficult. Flags are the most visible and emotive — but not necessarily the only — representation of what many in Northern Ireland hold so dear: sovereignty, allegiance, and identity. The text calls for a follow-on effort – a Commission on Identity, Culture, and Tradition – that would convene a public debate across Northern Ireland on such issues as flags, emblems, the role of the Irish language, and a Bill of Rights. The Commission would submit a report to the leaders of Northern Ireland with its recommendations. Despite our disappointment that more definitive prescriptions could not be agreed upon, I believe the Commission offers a pathway for meaningful progress and very much hope it is constituted.

Our mandate ran until December 31 – a deadline established by the Northern Ireland government – and at that point we ended the talks. Two of the parties – Sinn Fein and the Social Democratic and Labour Party – endorsed the text in its entirety. A third, Alliance, endorsed the part dealing with the past. The other two parties, the Democratic Unionist Party and the Ulster Unionist Party, decided not to endorse the text.

Some have interpreted this outcome as an indication that the agreement met more nationalist than unionist concerns. Both Professor O'Sullivan and I reject this characterization. There is a great deal in the proposal for unionists as well as nationalists. There is also a great deal in the text for the many in Northern Ireland who are not politically aligned but simply want to have a better understanding of the past and more reason to look forward to the future.

To be candid, however, the outcome was a disappointment. The draft reflects months of conversations with individuals and groups within Northern Ireland as well as the five parties. It reflects the often competing preferences of the five parties and what was required to bridge them. We understand that no party is fully comfortable with every element of the December 31 text. That should surprise no one. Politics inevitably requires that each party accept some elements it views as disagreeable in order to advance the greater good; indeed, it is only through compromise that the political parties will be able to collectively deliver the better future that the people of Northern Ireland demand and deserve. Here I can do no better than to quote Henry Kissinger, who in a recent and typically thoughtful assessment of the principles that would need to inform any diplomatic settlement in Ukraine, noted that the test of any proposed accord "is not absolute satisfaction but balanced dissatisfaction." I believe the December 31 Northern Ireland text met this test and then some, as its components should provide the basis not just for balanced dissatisfaction but balanced satisfaction.

Leaders must be prepared to take and make precisely this case to their constituents and the broader public. The true definition of leadership is a willingness to tell your supporters – not just your opponents – what they do not want to hear. A second requirement is to speak to those across the political divide, to reassure them that their core interests are not threatened and that what is in the interest of one party or group or tradition need not be inconsistent with the interests of the other. And in the case of Northern Ireland, there is a third requirement for leaders, as appropriate, to honestly acknowledge responsibility for the past.

I continue to believe that it is desirable for the parties to reach a comprehensive agreement covering all three issues; comprehensive agreement may also be necessary in order to accommodate tradeoffs and compromises. That said, it is ultimately up to the five parties to determine whether the ability to move ahead in any one area should be dependent upon consensus on the whole.

Over the past ten or so weeks, the parties have held a number of meetings in an effort to narrow their remaining differences and to add some needed detail, such as in the area of what would constitute a code of conduct for parades and protests. This effort, though, came to something of a halt two weeks ago when it was disclosed that the British government had sent letters to nearly 200 people assuring them that they were not wanted by the police.

Virtually all I know about these letters is what I have learned from public exchanges that have taken place over the past few weeks. The issue of "on the runs" (OTRs), involving individuals suspected of having committed paramilitary crimes or those who had been charged or convicted of such crimes and had escaped from prison, was referred to only tangentially in a few of the more than one hundred meetings that our team conducted over the six months of talks. The issue was never discussed in any detail. I had no idea of what was in the letters, how many were sent, or to whom. Nor was there any indication that anything mentioned in our presence was not known of and understood by all of Northern Ireland's political leaders.

It is my understanding from public reports that the letters essentially informed select individuals that there was insufficient evidence to pursue or prosecute them should they return to the United Kingdom. But it is also my understanding that the letters make clear that prosecution could come about if new information regarding violations of the law came to light. In short, the letters did not offer amnesty. I appreciate the forceful reactions that have come from political leaders in Northern Ireland who were not officially informed of these letters, but I see nothing in their content that would justify walking away from the process that all five parties have been involved in.

Like many others, I look forward to seeing the report about the OTR issue that Prime Minister Cameron has called for by the end of May. That said, I believe that these recent revelations and the reaction to them only reinforce the importance that the five parties continue to build on the progress made in the latter half of 2013 on matters relating to the past and other issues.

Where do things go from here? I have no crystal ball, but I agree with the First Minister when he says that the three issues at the center of the talks are issues that have to be dealt with. To this I would add a sense of urgency. The passage of time will not by itself heal Northern Ireland's society or make it more normal or bring it together. To the contrary, absent political progress, the passage of time will only create an environment in which social division intensifies, violence increases, investment is scared off, alienation grows, and the best and brightest leave to make their futures elsewhere.

Much of the world looks to Northern Ireland as a model of peacebuilding, and many in Northern Ireland like to be so viewed. But all this is premature. Yes, the society has come a long way from where it was two decades ago, but it still has a long ways to go before it can set an example others will want to emulate. It is up to the leaders of Northern Ireland to make politics work toward the objective of completing the peace process. The stakes are great. Largely depending upon what they choose to do, the future of Northern Ireland will either be that of a vicious circle or a virtuous one. I hope they make the right choice, and make it soon.

Thank you for this opportunity to be here today. I look forward to your questions.

Mr. SMITH. Ambassador Haass, thank you very much. And thank you for the enormous amount of time you have spent over the many years, including much of last year, in trying to cobble together a meaningful and responsive approach that will really take Northern Ireland forward and make progress.

You know, in her testimony in the third panel, Julia Hall from Amnesty International points out that the current mechanisms, while they have worked for some, have failed to conduct prompt, thorough and effective investigations in an independent and impartial manner in line with the UK's international human rights commitments. And she points out that repeated investigative failures across the mechanisms have crucially—I think she means critically, or maybe crucially—undermined confidence and trust in her ability to deliver the truth about the past; and secondly, points out that the mandates, there has been a piecemeal approach to investigations adopted in Northern Ireland.

It would appear that both Baroness O'Loan and you are both calling for a new, much more effective mechanism. And, again, I think many lawmakers and policymakers in this town have moved on to other things, the reason why this hearing has been convened.

Could you speak to those criticisms of the current mechanisms, while well-meaning, unwittingly have not produced the record of results that one would have hoped for? And then this whole idea of unfinished business. I would hope that some of our friends in the media today or even tomorrow, when they write their articles and publish their stories, would talk about the unfinished business. You have it in your report. I have read it. It is excellent. It makes so many very fine and, I think, very forward-thinking and very credible recommendations, yet most people don't even know about it.

Ambassador HAASS. Well, thank you, sir, for what you said. Just to be clear on one thing, it is not my report or our report.

Mr. SMITH. Good point.

Ambassador HAASS. It is a report that grew out of this process and our attempt to bridge the political divides, yet still put forward a set of ideas that, if adopted, we believe would leave Northern Ireland better off, considerably better off.

On your question, the current approaches, they are multiple. Essentially you have four existing approaches. They are time-consuming; the fact that we are still talking about unfinished investigations tells you that. They are in some cases extraordinarily expensive. In some cases they are quite distracting, because groups like the current police service have everyday tasks to carry out, yet they are still also obligated to deal with the heavy burden of the past. Plus, despite all this, despite all this effort and investment, some of the current efforts do not enjoy the kind of broad legitimacy that one needs if they are effectively to deal with the past.

So it is not a criticism about effort; it is not a criticism of motives; it is simply an observation, if you will, about results. And the reason, therefore, we came up with the idea of creating a new and independent Historical Investigations Unit with investigative powers was to try to deal with this, the fact that the current approaches were time-consuming, a bit of a distraction, and lacked legitimacy because they were seen as under the police service rather than distant from them.

So that is why we have come up with this approach, and we believe it is the best way of threading the needle. It is not, as the Baroness suggested, what has been put forward in this report, under the police service. That is simply incorrect. It is also independent.

Now, in a democracy—and we understand this from our own system; indeed, I used the analogy at times in the talks—we have things like the Supreme Court, we have the Federal Reserve, we have independent institutions. But in a democracy you still need accountability. You can't have free-floating institutions that don't have a degree of tether or of accountability, and therefore there has to be an appointments process. There has to be some oversight process in a democracy. And what we tried to do was come up with the best way we knew—in consultation with the five parties—of threading that needle, of coming up with something that was as independent as could possibly be construed or constructed, yet at the same time have adequate oversight and accountability, and we believe that what is in the December 31 text does exactly that.

On your larger point, and I tried to get to it in my remarks, when I was asked to do this, and I accepted it, a lot of people seemed surprised, and they seemed surprised back in New York or Washington, but also even in London. And everyone said, to a person, I thought this was resolved. Didn't you have the Good Friday or Belfast Agreement in 1998?

And what I believe that highlights, and you got at it in your opening statement, there is a difference between, if you will, ending a war and building a peace. Any society coming out of something like three decades of Troubles—and Mr. Rohrabacher talked about the Civil War in this country—any society like that is traumatized for obvious reasons. It is traumatized psychologically, physically, economically and politically. There are all sorts of divisions, wounds, damage and the like. And obviously Northern Ireland was no exception. One day North Korea will be no exception. I look forward that day happening when it gets out from under the rule and the division it has known.

And so what this showed to me is that even though Northern Ireland had emerged from the Troubles, and most of the violence had stopped, it had not become anything remotely like a normal society. If you walk down parts of Belfast, you were still confronted by concrete barriers separating communities. Upwards of 90 percent of the young people still go to divided schools, single-tradition schools. Neighborhoods are still divided.

I don't see the society sowing the seeds of its own normalization, of its own unity, if neighborhoods and schools are still divided. What worries me in that kind of environment, particularly where politics are not shown to be making progress, alienation will continue to fester, and violence, I fear, could very well reemerge as a characteristic of daily life.

So it is premature to put Northern Ireland, as much as we would like to, into the outbox of problems solved. I would love for it to be there, and I look forward to that day, but, quite honestly, it is not there yet.

Mr. SMITH. I thank you for that. I hope that that is a message that lawmakers and others will convey, especially at the end of the week when so many people will make their way from the Republic of Ireland and Northern Ireland as part of the St. Patrick's Day festivities, because, again, I think there is a superficial understanding about all done, as you put it, it is finished, time to move on, and we need, again, to redouble our efforts, again, to take your blueprint, and let people know that there is much more that needs to be done.

Let me just ask you, if you would like to respond to it, you know, the Finucane case, the horrible, horrific murder of Patrick Finucane. His wife, who is here, Geraldine, who was wounded, the family was all there, and they have on several occasions testified through our subcommittee in an appeal to the British Government, different Prime Ministers to finally do what they promised to do, and that is implement or create and implement a public inquiry.

Judge Cory sat where you sat, Ambassador Haass, and he couldn't have been more emphatic. He spoke for the better part of an hour, and he kept getting back to the unfinished business of the Finucane murder and the collusion that was inherent in it.

Would you want to speak to that? I mean, this is like one festering sore. I absolutely am in awe of the courage and the tenacity of Geraldine and her family in carrying on this call for an accountability. Would you want to respond to it?

Ambassador HAASS. I am happy to.

One has to be impressed by the courage of the Finucane family and by what they have had to endure. The report deals with the question of inquiries, but essentially leaves it to the British Government to make a decision as to whether it is or believes that is the best way to deal with the, as you describe it, unfinished business.

The bulk of the report is on other mechanisms for dealing with all sorts of situations that have never been investigated—still there are hundreds and hundreds of murders and deaths that have never been investigated, and in many cases where they have been investigated by whatever mechanism—there are multiple mechanisms, as you know, for investigating them—people are not satisfied with the results.

And we also create a mechanism where there is reason to do so for reopening certain things. So that is essentially the approach. But that will have to be a decision by the British Government, whether they believe that it is worth, from their point of view, going down the path of another inquiry.

Mr. SMITH. By having promised it, it is just we are looking for promise fulfilled.

Let me ask two final questions. Nuala O'Loan made a very strong point in both her oral and written testimony about the legacy unit. It seems to me that when you have former Special Branch officers in charge of what is allowed out and, you know, revealed versus what is not, that without some kind of oversight that is very real, that is an engraved invitation, it would seem to me, to just continue hiding a truth that may not be very pretty.

And secondly, with regards to the Military Reaction Force, as one of our witnesses Eugene Devlin, who was shot, and, as he says in his testimony, Daniel Rooney, age 18 like himself, was killed by a bullet, and the information now that is becoming much more visible about this Military Reaction Force. Your thoughts on that?

Ambassador HAASS. Well, again, that is why there are two new mechanisms that this report recommends. One is a Historical Investigations Unit, which would look at things through a legal lens; and then there is a separate information unit that would be created to encourage people to come forth, because as it turns out, there are a number of survivors and victims whose priority, if you will, is not necessarily in the legal realm, ''justice'' or punishment, but rather their priority is to simply find out what happened, to get the facts about what happened to a loved one. And there are certain incentives put forward in order to encourage individuals, organizations, and governments to cooperate with this information pathway.

Now, at the same time, there is nothing in the information pathway that provides amnesty; it simply provides what we would call limited immunity. So information introduced there cannot be used for prosecution, but if other information is somehow gained through other means, and that warrants prosecution, prosecution could still happen.

And I think it is important that governments, whether it is the British Government or the Irish Government, are involved in this process fully, and I believe that obviously paramilitary organizations need to be involved in this process, paramilitary or other organizations across the board, in no small part because the bulk of the violence was done at the hands of paramilitaries. But governments do have special obligations under European law, and obviously, I believe the British Government needs to be a participant in dealing with the past.

Can I say one other thing about it? Because it gets at Mr. Rohrabacher's comments.

Mr. SMITH. Sure.

Ambassador HAASS. The point of view he talked about, and I think the analogy you used was the scab. There is a point of view that echoes what he says, and it is the idea that in order to deal with the future, you have to let go of the past. There is that. And public figures and private figures in Northern Ireland do articulate that.

On the other hand, I came away persuaded that it wouldn't work in this case; that you would never get to the point of healing, in a sense, to use his analogy—and analogies are always dangerous, but I will use it—you would never form the scab without a process, you would never get to the point of healing, and that you needed a process.

And I came to this, by the way, after some of the most emotional meetings of my career, which was meeting with the victims and survivors and meeting with the families. And you can't emerge from these meetings and not be powerfully affected by it.

And when I met with these individuals, and I met more broadly with people in Northern Ireland, I came away persuaded that you needed a process that would deal with the past. We have talked about, too, a legal dimension; we have talked about also an information availability dimension.

There are other aspects as well. I think this society doesn't teach the past well. We need a curriculum that deals better with it. We need a museum. Why wouldn't there be somewhere a museum dedicated to the Troubles, not that you try to come to a common narrative. I, for one, believe that is unrealistic at this point given how divided the society is. But why couldn't you have a place where competing narratives are allowed, where people understand the facts, here is the timeline, here are the facts, and people can put forward different narratives?

But I do believe this is a society that will not be able to get beyond what it has gone through unless there is something of a political, but also psychological process of contending with it. Otherwise what will happen is different communities will live with their own versions of the past, and I came away thinking that there would never be the kind of bridge-building or normalization we and they want to see without a multidimensional approach to dealing with what happened.

Mr. SMITH. Mr. Keating.

Thank you very much.

Mr. KEATING. Thank you, Mr. Chairman.

At the outset, I do want to say this, that I will apologize. I have got dual responsibilities. I am managing the floor debate in just a short period of time. So in particular to Ms. Finucane and Mr. Devlin, I apologize if I am interrupted back and forth doing that, as well as to you, Dr. Haass.

Quickly, you mentioned the prospects of further violence. Although the political violence has declined significantly, and fatalities have almost been eliminated since the agreement, tensions remain strong between unionist and nationalist communities. Now, to what extent are paramilitary organizations on both sides still capable of disrupting the peace? What is your assessment of the risk of new outbreaks from these entities?

Ambassador HAASS. That is a question I ask myself a lot. I think there are two kinds of violence we have to worry about in Northern Ireland. You have got one, which is paramilitary violence. You still have so-called splinter groups on the so-called Republican side in the Northern Ireland context. And while I was there, there was more than one car bombing and so forth. There were some also letter bombs sent. So you still have that. And you still have paramilitary groups on the loyalist side who are in a position to carry out violence.

So I can't give you, if you will, a quantitative prediction. It is simply my sense that the possibility of a paramilitary violence is real, and then I want to come to the other form of violence which could affect it, which is political protests of various types. We have seen now a larger number of protests or marches or both where then you have had friction—I don't know any other word to use— with police forces. And you had a large number of policemen hurt over the last year as well as individuals. What worries me, then, is the possibility for this kind of violence to continue to get worse and whether the two kinds of violence could begin to affect one another.

If you begin to have greater violence at the political level, I worry that that creates a context in which then there could well be greater violence at the paramilitary level. Indeed, this is the history of Northern Ireland. Early on, before the Troubles in the early stage, you had political protest and violence, and then ultimately it led into a much more dangerous era of paramilitary violence, and I do not want to see history repeat itself.

Mr. KEATING. Your last comments actually are along the lines of one of my questions. The countries in Central and Eastern Europe have enjoyed mixed success in dealing with difficult historical issues, whether it is World War II or the Holocaust. In some cases, ostensibly independent institutions charged with historical investigations have been unduly politicized as a means of influencing public opinion, shaping political debate, or benefitting certain political actors or parties.

In other cases, in the case of Germany and Poland, academics and educators have successfully collaborated to develop historical curriculum taught in both countries that encourages students to critically consider competing historical narratives as a means of promoting reconciliation.

What are the prospects, long and short, about this? I am in no way equating the Holocaust or other things, because each instance and terrible instances in our history define themselves, but one of the lessons of that, really, has been informative. And I look at groups in the U.S., like Facing History and Ourselves and other groups from an academic standpoint that have done so much to foster a greater understanding. And you said maybe you never can get to full agreement on the issues that you discussed, but we can at least foster the kind of academic educational narrative that is important in this instance.

Ambassador HAASS. I think you are exactly right. I think some of it is going on, as best I can tell. You see it at the academic level; you see it even with some of these victims and survivor groups. A lot of these groups bring people together from different traditions.

One of the things that makes these meetings powerful is you have people who may have suffered at the hands of, say, a Republican paramilitary from the Provisional IRA, and people who suffered from a loyalist paramilitary, and then others who suffered then from the hands of that British troop. And there is an ability, in that case, to talk across certain divides.

I would simply say the academic approach has been limited. There is a lot more that could and should be done. I would like to see—how would I put it?—vehicles created where academics would come together. For example, I would like to see the leading historians of Northern Ireland come together to try to do what you suggest, to come up with a—if not a single history of the past, then a collective history, because, again, I think it is important that young people understand what happened, the reality of what happened.

Let me give you one reason. I don't want young people to only hear the story from one side, and I never want anyone to get caught up in the ''romance of it all.'' It would be a real tragedy if another generation of young people thought that ''fulfillment'' was to be found in the path of becoming a paramilitary. And it would be good if there was a place they could go to where they would see the costs to individuals and the society of that kind of an experience.

That can only happen if historians from the various traditions come together and try to produce a living, not just a physical, monument to the past. The shorthand we sometimes used was a ''museum of the history of the Troubles.'' Something like that, I believe, would be extraordinarily valuable.

Mr. KEATING. Just one more thought I had, and this is such a profound issue, and it works on so many levels. There are a couple of demographics that I just want to raise and see if you think at all this can foster a better relationship.

Number one, the remains of disparity and unemployment with Catholics that are much higher that are there, that, left unaddressed, and not having the so-called benefits of a peace dividend, I think—I just want to ask you what effect that will have. And number two, the other demographics are the population, the number of Irish people are—it is growing, and the Protestant people are diminishing somewhat, and then you have that shift that is going on there.

Will either of those things have an effect, positive or negative, on efforts to bring peace?

Ambassador HAASS. On the first point, which is unemployment, it is high among Catholics, as you say, but it is really high among poorly educated young people in both communities, which is one of the problems, because those are, if you will, the foot soldiers of some of the violence that we are seeing.

What this argues for is two things: One is specific projects that would employ people with their skill sets, and there are lots of ideas around for development. Indeed, there was one area where there was a big project that was put forward, and it couldn't go forward at what is called Maze Long Kesh because it is also the site where you have the prison and the hospital which was associated with where a lot of people were incarcerated during the Troubles, it was where Bobby Sands had his hunger strike, so it has taken on obviously a politicized position in Northern Ireland life.

But there are a lot of potential resources that could go to develop that area, put aside the question of what to do about the historic places, and a lot of young people can be employed. So projects linked to getting the communities working would be great.

The larger point, as my former boss Colin Powell used to say, is that capital is a coward. Investment in Northern Ireland has to compete with investment from everywhere else, and capital and investment will stay away from Northern Ireland if its future looks uncertain. So it is one of the reasons that it is important that politics advance, or, quite honestly, investors will take their dollars elsewhere.

In terms of population demographics, Protestants still now hold what I would call a plurality, as the most recent numbers I have seen are slightly below the majority. The Catholics' share is less than that, but it is slightly going up. And I think it obviously is part of the backdrop to this process. It is one of the reasons that people need to constantly reach across the community divide and not just speak to their own supporters, but to reassure people about the future.

You know, it is interesting; the document that brought us in here, that created this panel that I was asked to chair, the title of it was ''Together.'' And the whole idea was to create a Northern Ireland of a shared future. And it had all these grandiose plans. What is missing, 90 percent of life, as we used to teach, is implementation, and we need to see some of these plans for a shared future begin to be realized. But as long as people see separate futures, then it is going to be very hard to make the shorter progress that, in a sense, both communities, I believe, need.

Mr. KEATING. Great.

And just one more in the nature of comment, should I not be here for Ms. Finucane and Mr. Devlin's testimony, is that I must tell you as a former prosecutor and someone that was involved in our own State as chairman of judiciary, I do believe very strongly that going forward, if we are going to respect the rule of law, we have to have confidence going backwards that if there wasn't rule of law, that we do things to acknowledge that, correct that, because the message will be, well, the rule of law isn't something that transcends time. It is conveniently turned on and turned off. And I think the Commission's effort and those efforts to go back is important for the future to instill respect in that rule of law. So——

Ambassador HAASS. I am with you on that. I agree about the past, and I also agree with it about the present. One of the things that was a stumbling point was the idea to embed a code of behavior for all these marches and parades and attending protests and to embed it in the rule of law. And that is essential for a democratic society.

So I think it is true for the past; I think it is true for the present. Obviously, and you know better than I do, it has got to be administered fairly and efficiently and all that. But I believe a democratic society rests on it, and Northern Ireland can't be an exception.

Mr. KEATING. I yield back.

Mr. SMITH. Thank you, Mr. Keating.

Chairman Rohrabacher.

Mr. ROHRABACHER. Thank you very much.

Just before I go into questions, a little bit about a month ago I was called over to the Japanese Embassy, and I was asked to provide the toast to Japanese-American friendship, and I think it was the Emperor's birthday or something like that. And I did that, and I felt real good about it, and I knew my father would approve.

My father was a United States Marine in World War II, and how ironic that his son is at the Japanese Embassy providing a toast to the friendship between the Japanese people and the people of the United States. There was a lot of blood there, a lot of bloodshed in that relationship, not only U.S. Marines being killed, but hundreds of thousands of Japanese civilians being evaporated by our bombing, which was done in order to end that war, I understand.

But it seems to me that today, Japan and the United States have a wonderfully close friendship. We have had that for decades. And it is so difficult for me to see two people who are separated by their Christian religion not being able to come to have a greater peace than they have in Northern Ireland.

Let me ask you, and, by the way——

Ambassador HAASS. Can I say one thing?

Mr. ROHRABACHER. Yes. Go right ahead.

Ambassador HAASS. I apologize for interrupting.

What is interesting to me, though, about what you said, well, two things. One is one of the things we have called for in this report is not simply apologies, but acknowledgments, that people talk about their responsibility and role in the past.

Honesty will go a long way in Northern Ireland. The more honesty there is and people accepting personal responsibility, that kind of personal gesture, I believe, will have extraordinary impact. When we have seen it already, it has had extraordinary impact.

The other thing that came to mind what you were saying——

Mr. ROHRABACHER. Before you go on to your second point, I agree with you 100 percent in that I think that acknowledging one's faults, for that to have a positive result also has to have forgiveness. I mean, that is the other half of the equation. That is what Christ talks to us Christians about.

And excuse me. Go ahead.

Ambassador HAASS. The other thing—and I know before you were raising the question of the some of the dangers or risks of too much a focus on the past, but take another analogy from Asia. You used the one of the United States and Japan, but look at the Japanese-Korean relationship and the Japanese-Chinese relationship. They are increasingly—held back doesn't begin to get at it; poisoned might not be too strong of a word—by the legacy of the past.

And the fact that you have totally different perceptions and takes on the past, you teach it different ways in the schools, and it is both impressive and depressing how much of the current diplomacy is affected and limited by different perceptions of the past. So, again, to me that is a lesson about why sometimes you do need to deal with the past before you can effectively deal with the future.

Mr. ROHRABACHER. That is a very good point.

Let me ask you something about your knowledge, and, first of all, thank you for the wonderful work you have dedicated your life to, and it is something that is so admirable, that type of—what you are expending your energy or intellect and your time of your life being a peacemaker; as I say, blessed are the peacemakers, et cetera. And that is why we are so proud to work with Chairman Smith, because he has dedicated his life to these type of things as well.

Let me ask you about Ireland. Has there been any evidence that Protestants have been discriminated against in southern Ireland, in the regular part of Ireland?

Ambassador HAASS. In the Republic of Ireland?

Mr. ROHRABACHER. Yes.

Ambassador HAASS. I don't know the answer to that question about the state of Irish society. I have never heard of that recently.

Mr. ROHRABACHER. Yeah. I have never heard about it.

Ambassador HAASS. Yeah. I mean, the population of Ireland is also, I think—my numbers could be off here, but it is upwards of 97, 98 percent Catholic. So all I can say is I have not heard reports of that, but I could be—you know, I am certainly uninformed, and I could always be misinformed.

Mr. ROHRABACHER. I think there was a lot of arguments when Ireland was separating from British domination that the Protestants—there would be retaliation against the Protestants, and I didn't see it. I mean, I have studied—I love Ireland. I love the history and the culture, the music, and the beer. I just love Ireland, and I have studied a lot about it, and I didn't see any repercussions against the Protestants when the British left.

Now, I will say this: I personally believe the issue that we are talking about today would not exist had the British not "shnookered" the Irish into the original agreement to give up those five counties. The bottom of the line is Ireland is Ireland, and they are all Irish, and had that not—we wouldn't be facing this right now. And it is six counties, pardon me. I will leave the British with one.

But the fact is that perhaps today, perhaps the real solution lies— and from what I understand, there is only one county that has a very big majority of Protestants over Catholics. Maybe if we let these people have their right to self-determination via each county voting on it might lead to a restructuring of the whole sys- tem there, which might lead to a little better feelings after a period of time when people have to live together. That is just a thought.

But let's get to the question now. And the question is this: The Good Friday agreements happened in 1998.

Ambassador HAASS. Yes, sir.

Mr. ROHRABACHER. That is 15 years ago. And so it has been 16 years since the violence stopped.

Ambassador HAASS. For the most part.

Mr. ROHRABACHER. Okay. During that time period, I don't see anything wrong with people saying anyone held accountable for any acts of violence during this time when there wasn't official peace and people were negotiating it, I could understand that. But going back beyond the 16 years, the 16 years of peace, before that we just heard the Baroness talking about maybe giving people 2 years in prison for someone who was maybe in their twenties when something happened or thirties. Is that part of the plan for peace?

Ambassador HAASS. Well, again, two separate issues. One is the ability to prosecute, and the other is the question of what would be the penalty for those found guilty.

You know, I believe, again, Mr. Keating and I had this exchange, and I believe for democratic societies there needs to be the ability to prosecute for crimes for which there is no statute of limitations. I think that is true from a political and legal point of view.

I also came away from my experience here thinking that it is necessary politically and psychologically; that, again, for people to be open to a future, they have got to feel that the past has been fairly and comprehensively dealt with. And I don't believe that should be something, by the way, that individuals have the right——

Mr. ROHRABACHER. I don't know. I wish I could tell you that I believe in what you are saying, because I know that that is the theory that we can—something we can believe in that will create a better world. But, again, my father was a Marine in World War II. A member of our church, was my father's best friend, called me aside one Sunday and said, you know, I was in Guam, and we went out after the Japanese had surrendered, and there were little groups out there, and we surrounded a group of 13 of them, 13 or 14 of these Japanese, around a campfire one night, and we had a Japanese speaker with us. And we came out and we said, hands up, surrender, and they all did. And one of our guys just started shooting, then we all started shooting, and we killed all of them.

And I mean, that was an atrocity. And during the Battle of the Bulge, there is another case where I know of where our soldiers actually killed a lot of German soldiers, knowing full well the Germans were killing our soldiers, however.

It seems that if we are going to have a better world, we have got to recognize that those things are evil, and that evil does lurk among humankind, but that if we try to go back, I don't think it would be fair to that Marine to go back and then to charge him with a war crime. Do you?

Ambassador HAASS. I am uncomfortable commenting upon other situations, because I know enough to know that every situation stands on its own and is different and unique. I would simply say, though, one of the things you have to think about in the case of Northern Ireland is you are not thinking about two different countries, you are talking about a society that we want to be commingled, which is not divided.

And, again, I don't believe it is realistic to think that you will have a unified society if you have someone across the street living from someone else, and people know that this individual was involved in certain activities and that they lost a loved one because of it. I think you are expecting too much from human nature to think that—that people can get beyond that kind of an experience.

And, again, we may just simply disagree here. I am not sure it is healthy for a society to do that. I do think there has to be a sense of accountability and responsibility. Now, what Northern Ireland has tried to do is put certain ceilings in many cases on the jail penalty and time that individuals would have to serve. And I don't want to speak for anybody there, but my sense is that is the way they have tried to compromise this, to basically have prosecution continue where it is warranted, but also to have a degree of mercy, if you will, or limits on the penalties that would be incurred by individuals who committed crimes during the periods of the so-called Troubles. As you say, it is different after 1998.

So I think that has been the balancing act that people in Northern Ireland have had and more broadly have come up with there.

Mr. ROHRABACHER. Well, thank you very much. And I know I sound a little bit too idealistic here maybe, but I do think that forgiveness—if someone really has contrition, forgiveness goes a long way toward creating more peace in the world. Thank you.

Mr. SMITH. Thank you.

Ambassador HAASS. Thank you for what you said.

Mr. SMITH. I would just comment, if I could, very briefly. I will never forget, I was part of a reinterment ceremony at Srebrenica, with Reis Ceric, who was the Grand Mufti; Haris Silajdzic, who was President. And I remember hearing from widows who told me that there were people in the police to that day, this was 9 years ago, who were part of the genocide that was committed against, in that case, the Muslims who lived in Srebrenica, which was supposed to be a U.N. safe haven, and the horror that they felt knowing that in their police department sat someone in good standing still presumably meting out enforcement of law who had committed atrocities. And I think what we are trying to, and what you have done so well, and what others have done so well, is to say there is no statute of limitations for heinous crimes. There can be forgiveness, but that doesn't preclude justice, and justice means that there needs to be accountability.

And our biggest fear has been in the collusion side, and that is what got me into this, holding hearings, doing legislation that ensured that when certain people in the RUC came to the United States to get training at the academy, the police academy in Virginia, that they were fully vetted, because so many people had been just moved up, even got, we believe, moved up in rank and were grandfathered in. I mean, that was one of the flaws of the Patton Commission, that it grandfathered in, we believe, some people who had committed horrific acts of cruelty.

And just like with our own civil rights movement here, if you committed a crime, if you blew up an African American church and we find you, just like we will prosecute. And I think that is what we are trying to really—that message that there is no immunity for that kind of impunity. So I thank you.

Ambassador Haass, any final comment before we move on?

Ambassador HAASS. I would simply say that what was suggested in this report, this debate is a real debate. And that is why for certain families what was created was a path that would allow them simply to get information, and that people would then be encouraged to provide them information so they could psychologically and emotionally deal with what happened to their own families, and the person could know that that information itself would not be then handed over to authorities.

So it was not a ''prosecution first'' approach. We wanted to make sure that—on the other hand, we didn't want to preclude prosecution if that is what the state warranted was necessary, and if that information could be gotten through other means. That is the whole concept, as you know, of limited immunity.

So, again, all of this is a balancing act designed to ensure that certain principles are respected about the past and also continue to be respected in the present about the rule of law; yet also, to take into account the fact that there is, what, thousands and thousands and thousands, tens of thousands of individuals and families in Northern Ireland that have this tremendous burden of the past. And they have a special place in this society, and we wanted to give them a degree of choice in how they would pursue what it was they thought was necessary. And I never use the word ''closure.'' That sounds, I think, offensive for outsiders to say, but at least a degree of significant comfort with what happened.

So what was laid out was a set or a menu of possibilities, because there is no one single answer for every individual or every family. And what I think is in this—and, again, it was a collective effort, so I am not praising myself—but I actually think is a fairly unique approach, which is something, I believe, if adopted, would be very good for Northern Ireland and would be worthwhile for other societies that have gone through similar types of experiences to look at, a way of balancing individual needs and collective needs, as well as the past, the present and the future. And it is an attempt to come up with some trade-offs.

And I come back to Henry Kissinger's line, there is always going to be a balance of dissatisfactions, and that, to me, is the element of political possibility. But more positively, there is also a balance of satisfactions. In every side, if they look at what are the details of the past, if they look at what could be there with flags, or what is there with parading, there should be enough there that, if adopted, it would not hurt them politically, and it would help the society as a whole.

Those are two pretty good criteria, that they could politically manage it, and the society would be better off. And that is what we tried to do. We think the document does it. And we very much hope that people will come to that realization. There is no way to ultimately avoid these three issues, and there is no way you can or should in particular avoid the set of questions about the past. So I am very hopeful that it is a question of when and not if the political leaders of Northern Ireland come to that realization and then act on it. So, again, I appreciate what you all have done in this hearing by putting a spotlight on it. So thank you very much.

Mr. SMITH. And, again, the December 31 proposed agreement remains viable?

Ambassador HAASS. Absolutely.

Mr. SMITH. Great. Thank you.

Ambassador HAASS. Thank you, sir.

Mr. SMITH. Thank you very much, Ambassador Haass.

I would like to now invite our second panel, if they would make their way to the witness table, beginning first with Ms. Geraldine Finucane, wife of slain human rights attorney Patrick Finucane. As we all know, in 1990, loyalist government forced their way into her home and their home and murdered her husband Patrick Finucane, an Irish human rights lawyer.

She has advocated long and effectively for full disclosure of British state collusion in her husband's murder. She has been all over the world, including the United States many times, and including before this subcommittee and before Congress on several occasions.

Collusion in the Finucane murder remains one of the major unresolved questions in the peace process, and the peace process is an ongoing venture, and the British Government's refusal to fulfill its promise undermines that very process.

And, again, I want to welcome her and thank Geraldine for her unbelievable courage and tenacity.

We will then hear from Mr. Eugene Devlin, who was born and raised in Belfast. On the night of May 12, 1972, Mr. Devlin, with friends, went to a disco, and on their way home was shot by the British Army undercover unit, the Military Reaction Force, which was a covert, intelligence-gathering and counterinsurgency unit in Northern Ireland during the Troubles.

He later went to London to work, where the bar he was working in, it was bombed after 2 weeks. Mr. Devlin eventually came to the United States and today owns and operates a bar and restaurant in Red Bank, New Jersey. We had a very good conversation before the hearing, and, again, I thank him for coming and testifying about his ordeal and that of others who have been killed by the Military Reaction Force.

And then we will hear from Julia Hall, a human rights lawyer, Amnesty International's expert on criminal justice, counterterrorism and human rights in Europe. Her current work focuses on accountability of human rights violations in countries with a history of political violence, including Northern Ireland, and for violations committed in the context of the Global War on Terrorism.

Ms. Hall served on the research and editing team for a 2013 Amnesty International report on Northern Ireland and authored another research report on Northern Ireland that was published in 1997.

So, Geraldine, if you could all come. And as you physically come to the witness table, without objection, testimony from Anne Cadwallader and Alan Brecknell of the Pat Finucane Center will be made a part of the record as well as a submission from the Professor Patricia Lundy of the University of Ulster.

Ms. Finucane, if you can proceed.

Mr. Devlin, if you could please come on up, as well as Ms. Hall.

STATEMENT OF MS. GERALDINE FINUCANE, WIFE OF SLAIN HUMAN RIGHTS ATTORNEY PATRICK FINUCANE

Ms. FINUCANE. My name is Geraldine Finucane. My husband was Patrick Finucane, a Belfast solicitor murdered by loyalist paramilitaries on the February 12, 1989. My family and I have campaigned since the murder for a full public, independent judicial inquiry into the circumstances surrounding the killing. We have done so because of compelling evidence that his murder was part of a widespread British Government policy of collusion between the state and loyalist paramilitary.

Our suspicions, based on the evidence which has emerged over the last 25 years, received official confirmation in October 2011 when the Prime Minister David Cameron told us personally that on behalf of his government, he accepted that collusion was real and directly led to the murder of my husband.

The campaign has only had one objective from the outset: To discover and uncover the truth behind Pat's murder. From the very night that Pat was murdered, we knew the authorities were involved in some way, but we did not know the details. Pat had been subjected to constant threats from police officers during his professional career, threats made via his clients, threats that started as derogatory comments escalated into death threats.

Then, less than 3 weeks before his death, a government minister, Douglas Hogg, M.P., made a statement in the houses of Parliament that marked Pat and a small number of other solicitors for murder. He said, "I have to state that there are in Northern Ireland a number of solicitors who are unduly sympathetic to the cause of the IRA."

This comment was shocking and provocative. Hogg would not relieve why or from whom he had got information which could lead to such a statement being made. In later years we learned he had been briefed by senior members of the police.

Over many years my family and I persisted in seeking all the facts surrounding Pat's murder. This followed much investigation, lobbying, and speaking out at every opportunity. We have been assisted and supported by so many, yourselves included, who concern themselves with human rights in Ireland. All who have examined the case have been unequivocal in their demand that a public inquiry is necessary.

We persisted, and despite much deliberate delay, the British Government were finally forced to announce that an inquiry would be held. In 2001, the British and Irish Governments held talks at Weston Park, and one of the agreements to emerge was that an international judge would be appointed to look at six cases, and if he finds an inquiry necessary in any of the cases, the relevant government would agree to hold the inquiry.

Judge Peter Cory, a retired Supreme Court judge of Canada, was appointed, and in Pat's case, his report said,

> "The documents and statements I have referred to in this review have a cumulative effect. Considered together, they clearly indicate to me that there is strong evidence that collusive acts were committed by the Army, the Force Research Unit and RUC Special Branch and the Security Services. I am satisfied that there is a need for a public inquiry."

In reply to this report, the British Government once again delayed, and eventually they put in place new legislation, the Inquiries Act 2005. Although the legislation did need modernized, we took particular exception to one clause.

This gives a government minister the power to effectively control the flow of information. This power was called restriction notices. It allows the government power to dictate to the inquiry, what information is released even if the tribunal itself is in disagreement with that decision. This undermining of the judicial process drew much criticism. We felt we could not take part in such a process. We wanted and still want one inquiry that is open and fair and which gives a chance at reaching the truth.

So at this stage in our campaign, we reached an impasse; however, in 2010, there was a change of government and the new Secretary of State, Owen Paterson, met with us in November of that year. He told us his government was committed to resolving the case; delay suited no one. We were encouraged.

What followed was a year of meetings between our legal teams, signs were encouraging, and at no stage was an alternative to an inquiry ever discussed. So in late summer of 2011, when the Prime Minister asked to meet us, we were encouraged. In a telephone conversation between a senior Northern Ireland office official and my lawyer, Peter Madden, we were told we would be happy with what the Prime Minister would offer. We assumed this confidence would be a reflection of the position we had outlined over the previous year. How wrong we were. David Cameron stated he was ordering another paper review, an exercise similar to that carried out by Judge Cory. It was a meeting I shall never forget.

Whilst this review was limited in its powers and private in nature, it has revealed some very shocking information about methods employed by the security forces. It has provided many more questions and, indeed, reinforced the need for a public inquiry.

An inquiry into the murder of Pat Finucane will not solve the current re-emerging problems in Northern Ireland, but it would be a first step in restoring public confidence in our society. Until such time as the British Government lives up to the promise it made to my family, I will not give up my fight to expose the truth, and I take great encouragement as I look around this room today that the fight will be far from a lonely one.

Thank you so much for this opportunity to put my case on record.

Mr. SMITH. Thank you so very much, Mrs. Finucane, for your testimony and, again, for your dogged determination to get to the bottom of who or how many and who was in collusion with killing your husband. Thank you.

[Ms. Fincuane did not submit a prepared statement.]

Mr. SMITH. Mr. Devlin.

STATEMENT OF MR. EUGENE DEVLIN, VICTIM OF THE MILITARY REACTION FORCE

Mr. DEVLIN. Ladies and gentlemen, my name is Eugene Devlin, and today I am a proud American citizen, having made my home in this fine country since 1978. I am in the business of owning and operating restaurants. The opportunity to participate in this legislative process through this hearing is very much appreciated.

I was born in Ireland in 1954 in Andersonstown, a suburb of Belfast, County Antrim, in the province of Ulster. The recent Northern Ireland Troubles erupted during my teenage years. I had neither art nor part in the Troubles, but on the night of 12th of May 1972, the Troubles came to me, up close and personal.

Returning by cab from a school disco, with my friend Aiden MacAloon, I had failed to notice a car following us, nor did I notice that the car's unusual turn illuminated us with its headlamps. We were nearly home and on familiar turf. Suddenly a number of shots rang out and I fell wounded, whilst my companion managed to get over a hedge. My left arm was shattered by what I was later told was a 9-millimeter bullet, fired from a British Sterling automatic submachine gun. I was first taken to the Royal Victoria Hospital and then transferred, under heavy guard, to the military wing of the Musgrave Park Hospital. After surgery, I spent about a year with my arm in a cast, followed by months more in a sling.

Although they identified the bullet and the type of gun, they would not allow me to keep the bullet, as they required it for evidence. Although the 9-millimeter is a deadly force, had the bullet been a caliber .45 ACP from a Thompson submachine gun or a high velocity rifle bullet, I would probably not be here to testify today. Providentially, my arm saved my life, but today I still have the physical reminders of that wound and every day carry medication as a consequence.

Police forensics determined that neither my friend nor I had handled any weapons that night, nor have either of us ever been charged with any of the violations of law. Later that fateful night, a second, separate, such predatory, plain clothes car patrol fired on a group of equally innocent men, wounding five and killing Patrick McVeigh.

Rumors had been circulating about such death squads and random killings presumably to terrorize the population, but until that night, they were not uppermost in my mind. On September 27, 1972, Daniel Rooney, also aged 18—like myself, was killed by a similar bullet in a drive-by shooting, which differed from my situation only in that the perpetrators achieved a more deadly result.

It was a shock that someone who didn't know me would try to kill me, they nearly did, but I am sure they didn't care if I died any more than they cared about Patrick McVeigh or about Daniel Rooney. These shootings were unjustified and remain unjustifiable.

It was only later that it came out that these shootings were clandestine acts of a secret terrorist force carefully selected from the British Army, perhaps calculated to stimulate inter-communal retaliation, divide and conquer, among the various Irish communities. It seems they were part of the secret Military Reaction Force (MRF).

The most disturbing thing about this is that the Army, which had been sent in in 1970 to restore order and to protect us from sectarian or other violence, had become transformed into an army of occupation, with elements of that Army operating outside even their own law and regulations.

When the facts of these atrocities became public, those in whose interest, and presumably by whose orders, they were perpetrated disavowed any knowledge of specific irregularities. Their records are nowhere to be found, yet at the time, Prime Minister Heath ordered that the MRF cease and be disbanded; meanwhile, the perpetrators have generally been rewarded with pensions, promotions, and medals. There is a message in that.

Being shot that night in 1972 was a terrifying experience. The only other truly terrifying experience of my life was 9/11 in New York City, when I emerged from the subway station very near the World Trade Center 2 just as the building was collapsing. In both cases, I was an involuntary victim, but the difference in 9/11 was that even though I was still terrified, like so many others, I took the opportunity to become an instant voluntary responder, making it to my own restaurant on Pearl Street, a block or so from Fraunces Tavern, and working with my staff to provide aid and comfort to many people. Apart from having a terrifying experience, the only other similarities are that I wound up in hospital that night and also continue to suffer physical effects from the experience.

In the interests of truth and justice, I thank you for this opportunity to testify, and I would be happy to answer any of your questions.

Mr. SMITH. Thank you so very much, Mr. Devlin, for your testimony.

[The prepared statement of Mr. Devlin follows:]

"The Northern Ireland Peace Process:
Attempting to Deal with the Past"
Subcommittee on Africa, Global Health,
Global Human Rights, and International Organizations
Testimony of Eugene Devlin
March 11, 2014

Ladies and gentlemen: My name is Eugene Devlin, and today I am a proud American citizen, having made my home in this fine country since 1978. I am in the business of owning and operating restaurants. This opportunity to participate in the legislative process, through this hearing, is very much appreciated.

I was born in Ireland, in 1954, in Andersonstown, a suburb of Belfast, County Antrim in the Province of Ulster. The recent "Northern Ireland" Troubles erupted during my teen-age years. I had neither art nor part in the Troubles, but on the night of the 12th of May 1972, the Troubles came to me – up close and personal.

Returning by cab from a school disco, with my friend Aiden MacAloon, I had failed to notice a car following us, nor did I notice that car's unusual turn, illuminating us with its headlamps. We were nearly home, and on familiar turf. Suddenly a number of shots rang out, and I fell wounded, whilst my companion managed to get over a hedge. My left arm was shattered by, what I was later told, was a 9mm bullet, fired from a British "Sterling automatic" sub-machine gun. I was first taken to the Royal Victoria Hospital, and then transferred, under heavy guard, to the military wing of the Musgrave Park Hospital. After surgery I spent about a year with my arm in a cast, followed by months more in a sling. Although they identified the bullet and the type of gun, they would not allow me to keep the bullet, as they required it for "evidence." Although the 9 mm is deadly force, had the bullet been a caliber .45 ACP from a Thompson submachine gun, or a high velocity rifle bullet, I probably would not be here to testify today.

Providentially, my arm saved my life. But today I still have physical reminders of that wound, and every day, carry medication as a consequence.

Police forensics determined that neither my friend nor I had handled any weapons that night – nor have either of us ever been charged with any violation of law.

Later that fateful night, a second, separate, such predatory, plain-clothes car patrol fired on a group of equally innocent men, wounding five, and killing Pat McVeigh.

Rumors had been circulating about such death squads, and random killings, presumably to terrorize the population. But, until that night, they were not uppermost in my mind.

On 27th September 1972, Daniel Rooney (also age 18, like myself) was killed by a similar bullet in a drive-by shooting, which differed from my situation only in that the perpetrators achieved a more deadly result.

It was a shock that someone who didn't know me would try to kill me (they nearly did), but I am sure that they didn't care if I died, any more than they cared about Pat McVeigh, or about Dan Rooney. These shootings were unjustified, and remain unjustifiable.

It was only later that it came out that these shootings were the clandestine acts of a secret terrorist force, carefully selected from the British Army (perhaps calculated to stimulate inter-communal retaliation – "divide and conquer" – among the various Irish communities). It seems that they were part of the secret "Military Reaction Force" (MRF).

The most disturbing thing about this is that the army, which had been sent in, in 1970, to restore order, and to protect us from sectarian (or other) violence, had become transformed into an army of occupation, with elements of that army operating outside even their own law and regulations.

When the facts of these atrocities became public, those in whose interest (and, presumably, by whose orders) they were perpetrated, disavowed any knowledge of specific "irregularities." The records are nowhere to be found. Yet at the time Prime Minister Heath ordered that the MRF cease and be disbanded. Meanwhile, the perpetrators have generally been rewarded with pensions, promotions and medals. There is a message in that.

Being shot that night in 1972 was a terrifying experience. The only other truly terrifying experience of my life was "9/11" in New York City, when I emerged from the subway station very near to World Trade Center 2, just as the building was collapsing. In both cases I was an involuntary victim, but, the difference in 9/11 was that, even though still terrified, like so many others, I took the opportunity to become an instant voluntary responder – making it to my own restaurant on Pearl Street (a block or so from Fraunces Tavern) and working with my staff to provide aid and comfort to many people. Apart from having a terrifying experience, the other similarities are that I would up in hospital that night, and also continue to suffer physical effects from the experience.

In the interest of Truth and Justice, I thank you all for this opportunity to testify, and I'll be happy to answer your questions.

Mr. SMITH. Ms. Hall.

STATEMENT OF MS. JULIA HALL, EXPERT ON CRIMINAL JUSTICE AND COUNTER-TERRORISM IN EUROPE, AMNESTY INTERNATIONAL

Ms. HALL. Thank you, Chairman Smith, for this opportunity. It is nice to see you again. I am here to testify on behalf of Amnesty International.

Mr. Chairman, last November, the New York Times opined that although "much good in safety and sanity has flowed from the Good Friday Agreement, there is no need to draw a curtain on a lethal past that clearly remains deeply relevant for the people of Northern Ireland."

This editorial was in response to the suggestion that perhaps there should be no more investigations into crimes committed in the course of "the Troubles." Recognizing very real human suffering that people had endured, however, the Times quoted Amnesty International's Patrick Corrigan, who is here with us today, who said that such a cap on accountability was "an utter betrayal of victims' fundamental right to access to justice."

Mr. Chairman, the signing of the Good Friday Agreement in April 1998 signaled a turning point in the history of Northern Ireland, and there is no doubt that 15 years on, remarkable progress has been made in moving toward a more peaceful future; however, the ongoing failure to deal with Northern Ireland's difficult past has had negative consequences for both individuals and society at large.

Many families from across communities in Northern Ireland are still searching for truth, justice and accountability. The legacy of the past, however, affects not just individual victims, but society as a whole. Writing in The American Scholar in 2011, Duke professor Robin Kirk noted, "Belfast is one of the most segregated cities in the the world . . . a landscape of interfaces and peace walls that have grown higher, longer and more numerous since the Good Friday Agreement."

The Good Friday and subsequent agreements simply did not provide the tools or create the bodies or processes to fully grapple with the pain, anger and hurt that are inevitably the legacy of decades of violence and conflict.

In September 2013, Amnesty International issued a report titled, Northern Ireland: Time to Deal With the Past. I would ask that this report be made part of the record, Mr. Chairman.

Mr. SMITH. Without objection.

Ms. HALL. Thank you.

This report assessed the five existing mechanisms for dealing with the past in Northern Ireland, you have heard what those mechanisms are today, but I must say, we were deeply, deeply disappointed, dismayed in fact at what we found in the course of our research.

We have identified two key problems with the current approach. First, these bodies or processes have failed in the main to conduct prompt, thorough and effective investigations in an independent and impartial manner, in line with the United Kingdom's international human rights commitments.

54

The second, more pressing, point is that even if all of these mechanisms were operating at full steam in full compliance with their mandates, the piecemeal approach to them is too diffuse to provide a comprehensive picture of all the violations and abuses that occurred. As a result, much of the truth remains hidden, while those in positions of responsibility consequently have remained shielded.

Moreover, and this is a critical point, the focus on individual cases has limited the possibility for thorough examinations of patterns of abuse that occurred in the course of the conflict. For example, patterns of abuses by armed groups remain woefully under-investigated. Likewise, the role and actions of particular UK State actors have also not been subject to effective investigation. For instance, State collusion with Republican and loyalist armed groups is one of the critical issues that has yet to be addressed effectively by any of the existing mechanisms. Even in the few cases where the government has acknowledged that collusion has occurred, as in the case of Patrick Finucane, the victim's family still do not have the full truth and no one in higher levels of government has been held accountable.

Our report concluded that one overarching mechanism should be established to address the past in a comprehensive manner. It needs to be victim focused, empowered to investigate both individual cases and patterns of abuse, and where sufficient evidence exists, there needs to be the possibility of bringing to justice those responsible.

Thus, Amnesty International believes that the Haass draft proposals on dealing with the past are a step forward. The proposals will need to be refined to ensure that these mechanisms operate in compliance with international human rights standards, but they do provide a solid basis from which to proceed.

It is crucial that all the stakeholders in a peaceful Northern Ireland do not let yet another opportunity for progress slip by, due to lack of political will and vision. Amnesty International is deeply concerned, however, that the Haass proposals on dealing with the past may be held hostage to the lack of agreement on other contentious and sensitive issues or may fall victim to inaction in the face of other disagreements among the parties. We have urged the Northern Ireland's political parties and the UK and Irish Governments to take the proposals on the past forward as matter of urgency.

And finally, the U.S. Government and other U.S. political actors have an incredibly important role to play at this critical juncture. We urge the friends of Northern Ireland among you to call for real progress on delivering a comprehensive approach to the past.

As the Haass draft agreement itself emphasizes, the time to rise to the challenge of the past is now, because Northern Ireland does not have the luxury of putting off this difficult but potentially transformative task any longer.

Thank you.

Mr. SMITH. Ms. Hall, thank you very much for your testimony and for your report, which is very, very disturbing, but we need to know what is going on, we need to know the truth, and for asking very tough questions.

[The prepared statement of Ms. Hall follows:]

Joint Committee Briefing and Hearing:
"The Northern Ireland Peace Process Today: Attempting to Deal with the Past"

House Committee on Foreign Affairs
Subcommittee on Africa, Global Health, Global Human Rights, and International Organizations
Subcommittee on Europe, Eurasia, and Emerging Threats

11 March 2014

Written Statement
Julia Hall
Expert on Criminal Justice and Counter-Terrorism
Amnesty International

Mr. Chairman, and members of both subcommittees, thank you for holding this important and timely hearing and for inviting me to testify today on behalf of Amnesty International.

Mr. Chairman, last November the *New York Times* opined that although much "good in safety and sanity has flowed from the Good Friday Agreement," there is "no need to draw a curtain on a lethal past that clearly remains deeply relevant for the people of Northern Ireland." This editorial was in response to the notion that perhaps there should be no further investigations or prosecutions for crimes committed in the course of the Troubles. Recognizing the very real human suffering that people had endured, however, the Times' editorial board quoted Amnesty International's Patrick Corrigan, who said that such a cap on accountability was "an utter betrayal of victims' fundamental right to access to justice."

The people at this table and Baroness O'Loan have worked tirelessly to get at the truth and to give victims and survivors of the political violence in Northern Ireland such a route to justice. Special recognition must be given as well to the nongovernmental organizations who have worked with the families of individuals killed in the course of the violence and those who have been injured. Northern Ireland is richly endowed with a vibrant civil society composed of many organizations focusing on these victims' needs; they play a vital role, one that has helped keep alive the search for truth, accountability, and effective redress for victims and their families.

Mr. Chairman, the signing of the Good Friday Agreement on April 10th, 1998 signalled a turning point in the history of Northern Ireland and there is no doubt that fifteen years on, remarkable progress has been made in moving towards a more peaceful future. However, the ongoing failure to deal with Northern Ireland's shared, but difficult past has had consequences for both individuals and society-at-large. At the individual level, decades after their relatives were killed and after 15 years of relative peace, many families from across communities in Northern Ireland are still searching for the truth and for justice and for accountability. The legacy of the past, however, affects not just individual victims, but society as a whole. The failure to grapple with the legacy of the past has created fertile ground for continued division and mistrust, undermining progress towards a shared future. Writing in The American Scholar in 2011, Duke

University Professor Robin Kirk noted that "Belfast is one of the most segregated cities in the world, an occasionally Molotov-cocktail bombed landscape of 'interfaces' and 'peace walls' that have grown higher, longer, and more numerous…since the Good Friday Agreement."

The Good Friday and subsequent agreements, in taking on the huge and important work of building new political institutions, did not provide the tools or create the bodies or processes to fully grapple with the pain, anger, and hurt that are inevitably the legacy of decades of violence and conflict. The piecemeal, ineffcient and most importantly ineffective bodies currently tasked with dealing with the past have not proven equal to the task. This failure to establish a process that complies with international human rights standards lies squarely at the feet of the UK government, which has avoided the issue of accountability to serious negative effect. As a result, the past continues to haunt Northern Ireland's government, institutions, and people, creating division and mistrust that will undoubtedly set the stage for more conflict.

In 2012, Amnesty International decided to take the opportunity of the then-impending fifteen year anniversary of the Good Friday Agreement to examine what mechanisms existed in Northern Ireland to investigate past human rights abuses by non-state actors and violations by the state. We subsequently released the first major research report on Northern Ireland by an international human rights organization in over a decade. Titled "Northern Ireland: Time to Deal with the Past," this September 2013 report assessed these investigatory bodies -- the Historical Enquiries Team (HET), the Office of the Police Ombudsman for Northern Ireland (OPONI), the Police Service of Northern Ireland (PSNI), select coroner's inquiries, and public inquiries, such as the one Geraldine Finucane has been fighting for for 25 years -- in light of international human rights law and standards, and the degree to which they were delivering justive and redress for victims. We were deeply disappointed with what found.

I respectfully request that the report, copies of which we have available here today, be formally entered into the record.

In the course of our research, Amnesty International representatives interveiwed dozens of victims and their families, from across the community – Catholic and Protestant, Nationalist and Unionist, Loyalist and Republican, and unaligned. And while each person had his or her own story and perspective, there was a common clarion call among the majority for political leaders to give greater priority to victims' quests for truth, justice, acknowledgment and support. As one family member told us, "It's a good thing there is peace. We suffered…but I still want to know the truth about what happened to my son; and I want the world to know what happened in Northern Ireland."

The central overarching finding from our research, however, is that the approach to dealing with the past in Northern Ireland is not adequate; it too often has let victims down and critically, it does not fulfil the United Kingdom's human rights obligations. We have identified two key problems with the current approach. The first is at the level of the individual mechanisms that have been established or directed to investigate past violations and abuses. Victims and families who engaged with these mechanisms reported a range of experiences. Although some reported that these mechanisms have worked adequately in their specific case and delivered a satisfactory report, by and large those we interviewed told us how these bodies or processes have failed to conduct prompt, thorough and effective investigations in an independent and impartial manner, in line with the UK's international human rights commitments. Repeated investigative failures across the mechanisms have crucially undermined confidence and trust in their ability to deliver the truth about the past.

The second more pressing point is that even if all these mechanisms were operating in full compliance with their mandates, the piecemeal approach to investigations adopted in Northern Ireland is too diffuse to provide a comprehensive picture of all the violations and abuses that occurred during the decades of political violence. As a result, much of the truth remains hidden, while those in positions of responsibility consequently have remained shielded. These limitations have also contributed to a failure to develop a shared public understanding and recognition of the abuses committed by all sides. Moreover, the near singular focus on the investigation of killings and suspicious deaths has also meant that people who were injured as a result of life-threatening attacks or who were subjected to torture and other ill-treatment have virtually been excluded.

The mechanisms' focus on individual cases has limited the possibility for thorough examinations of patterns of abuses and violations that occurred during the conflict. For example, although armed groups were responsible for the vast majority of deaths and other human rights abuses, the details of their operations remain unclear and under-investigated. There needs to be a more thorough and comprehensive approach to the investigation of abuses by armed groups, into their institutional culture, and their policies and practices. Where there is solid evidence, those allegedly responsible for crimes must be held accountable in full and fair trials.

The role and actions of particular UK state bodies and agencies have also not been subject to effective investigation, nor has sufficient scrutiny been given to the investigation of state policy or state-sanctioned practices and whether they deliberately or indirectly gave rise to unlawful conduct. For instance, state collusion with Republican and Loyalist armed groups is one of the critical issues that has yet to be addressed effectively by existing mechanisms, and as a result, key questions remain regarding the degree and level of collusion that took place. Even in the few cases where the government has acknowledged that collusion occurred, as in the case of Patrick Finucane, the victims' families still do not have the full truth – and no one in higher levels of government has been held accountable.

Our report concludes that one overarching mechanism should be established to address the past in a comprehensive manner. We emphasize that it should be victim-focused and, among other things, empowered to investigate individual cases and patterns of abuses and violations; and where sufficient evidence exists there should be the possibility of bringing those responsible to justice. It should have powers to compel witnesses and documents, and be able to make recommendations aimed at securing full reparation for victims. We believe that such a mechanism would be an important step toward the currently existing environment of impunity for human rights violations and abuses in Northern Ireland, and allow for public recognition and understanding about the harm that was inflicted by all sides, and thus, possibly, set the stage for healing.

As you have heard today, Mr. Chairman, in September 2013 the five Executive parties in Northern Ireland began talks, chaired by Dr. Haass, in relation to three issues of contention, including how to deal with the past. Although Dr. Haass still awaits consensus by the parties with respect to his recommendations, Amnesty International believes that the Haass draft proposals on dealing with the past – specifically the proposals to establish two new mechanisms, the Historical Investigation Unit (HIU) and the Independent Commission for Information Retrieval (ICIR) – are a positive step forward. The proposals will need to be refined to ensure that these mechanisms operate in compliance with international human rights standards, but they provide a solid basis from which to proceed with efforts to deliver truth and justice for victims and their families.

Crucially, however, these draft proposals at the moment remain just that – draft proposals. It is crucial that all the stakeholders in a peaceful Northern Ireland do not let yet another opportunity for progress slip by due to lack of political will and vision. The Haass proposals represent a sensible and forward looking approach, with the promise to deliver truth and justice for victims and their families. Amnesty International is deeply concerned, however, that the Haass proposals on dealing with the past may be held hostage to the lack of agreement on other contentious and sensitive issues, or may fall victim to inaction in the face of other disagreements among the parties. Amnesty International has urged the Northern Ireland political parties, and the UK and Irish governments, to play their part in taking the proposals on the past forward as a matter of priority.

And a final call, Mr. Chairman, to the government of the United States, which was a key actor in helping to broker the Good Friday Agreement and remains to this day one of the custodians of the peace in Northern Ireland. The US government and other US political actors, many of whom sit on the two subcommittees sponsoring this hearing, have an incredibly important role to play at this critical juncture. We urge the friends of Northern Ireland among you to call for real and substantial progress on delivering a comprehensive approach to the past. As the Haass draft Agreement itself emphasizes, the time to rise to the challenge of the past is now, because *"Northern Ireland does not have the luxury of putting off this difficult, but potentially transformative, task any longer."*

Thank you.

———————

Mr. SMITH. Your point that no one at higher levels of government have been held accountable, I mean, that is appalling. That this many years into the process, that that remains the case, and the mistreatment of the Finucane family by the British Government is symptomatic of a larger problem, but certainly for their sakes, it is just a nightmare that just never ends.

I would like to ask you, if I could, Ms. Finucane, a couple of questions.

You know, I know you have a legal challenge to the Government's refusal to order an independent judicial inquiry into the state collusion of your husband's death. Could you give us an update as to where that is?

Ms. FINUCANE. Yes. After the Prime Minister announced that there would be a review, and we felt that, because we have been promised an inquiry it was the wrong decision, so we took proceedings in Belfast in the high court and to review the decision to have a review and not an inquiry, and that has taken slightly longer than we anticipated because they have been very slow at disclosing information, but at the same time it has been valuable, because much new information, even more information than came out in the DeSilva Report has come to light, and one of the interesting things was that the decision was not a unanimous decision made by the cabinet.

One of the chief civil servants was appalled that David Cameron could renege on the governmental promise made at Weston Park. He was astounded that David Cameron was going to announce a review and not an inquiry.

So we hope that the full hearing will start perhaps in the autumn, but we have to wait and see.

Mr. SMITH. Has either President Obama or the Prime Minister of the Taoiseach, Kenny, supported your efforts by urging Prime Minister Cameron to reconsider his decision, not to conduct the promised inquiry? Have either of them spoken out specifically on your case to Cameron for such an inquiry?

Ms. FINUCANE. Well, many years ago when the President was a Senator, he signed a Senate Resolution agreeing that we needed a public inquiry, and I know that the Taoiseach, Enda Kenny, continually brings up the case.

Mr. SMITH. Yes.

Ms. FINUCANE. And, whenever he can and wherever he can, and his support is invaluable.

Mr. SMITH. Now, but has President Obama? You said Senator Obama. Has——

Ms. FINUCANE. But——

Mr. SMITH [continuing]. President Obama?

Ms. FINUCANE. I don't know.

Mr. SMITH. Okay. Let me ask you this: Sir Jeremy Heywood, a member of Prime Minister Cameron's cabinet, has questioned the Prime Minister as to whether it was right to renege on a commitment to the inquiry, that he characterized the killing and collusion as a "dark moment in the country's history." Did that give you some encouragement to have someone of such high stature bucking the boss, so to speak?

Ms. FINUCANE. Well, yes. And he was not the only one and it wasn't a lone voice in the cabinet, but he has served more than one Prime Minister, so he is a very senior civil servant.

Mr. SMITH. Can I ask you, Mr. Devlin, has any representative of the British Government at any time ever apologized to you——

Mr. DEVLIN. Never.

Mr. SMITH [continuing]. For the terrible——

Mr. DEVLIN. Never.

Mr. SMITH [continuing]. Attack on you? Never.

Mr. DEVLIN. Never.

Mr. SMITH. Do you know what the current status of the investigation into the Military Reaction Force is? I mean, has anybody contacted—I mean, you are a victim.

Mr. DEVLIN. Yes.

Mr. SMITH. You are now here in America, but you are easily reachable, it would seem to me.

Mr. DEVLIN. No one has contacted me and I don't think there is anything being done, which is an absolute disgrace.

Mr. SMITH. Which again goes to Ms. Hall's point about no one in higher levels of government have been held to account. Perhaps you might want to elaborate on that, if you would, and whether or not the MRF has been included in at least a request that has been made for accountability by the British Government?

Ms. HALL. If you will permit me to take a step—one step back and talk about a report that was issued in July 2013 by Her Majesty's Inspectorate of the Constabulary.

This report found that the HET, the currently existing Historical Enquiries Team, treated cases where State actors were involved in killings very differently than they treated other cases. This is an official report, by the way, it is not the report of a non-governmental organization, although I do find NGO reports very credible. It was striking to see Her Majesty's Inspectorate say that in cases where British military officers or other State actors were involved, the HET was less rigorous in its inquiry, that various forms of evidence were made available to these actors prior to their giving statements in the HET, and this led the HMIC, to conclude that there is a serious undermining of confidence in the Historical Enquiries Team.

Now, that context for this notion, that people in higher levels of government have not been held accountable. State actors in general, in this process, have evaded accountability, and that is exactly why at this point, at this very critical 15-year-on juncture, Baroness O'Loan, Dr. Haass, Amnesty International, many other NGO's, and certainly the NGO's who are working with victims every single day on the ground in Northern Ireland, are calling for a comprehensive approach.

In a comprehensive approach where there is one mechanism that is looking at these cases, we could only hope that the force that held Mr. Devlin as a victim would definitely be a force that would be under investigation. Currently, to our knowledge, it is not under investigation in any way in the currently existing mechanisms.

So I hope that you can take that context and really understand very clearly that it is not an accident that higher level State actors are not being held accountable, it is not a simple oversight that this unit has never been under investigation. It is a deliberate policy of the Government of the United Kingdom to ensure that certain truths never are revealed about those years of conflict.

What they don't understand is the will of the families like the Finucanes, like Mr. Devlin, like the families that we have talked to, dozens and dozens of them over 2 years of research, these families are demanding justice and accountability. And I hope that the British Government is listening, because I don't think at this point in time, that their voices are going to be able to be drowned out any longer.

Mr. SMITH. In your view, has the Obama administration raised this in the way that it ought to?

Ms. HALL. We are here today to ask them to do so. We are here today to ask the United States Government to do precisely that, to ask other politicians like yourselves to do that. There are very few governments that have the kind of influence on the Government of the United Kingdom that the United States Government has. This is the forum where we are making that request of the U.S. Government, of President Obama, Vice President Biden and politicians in both houses of Congress.

Mr. SMITH. Let me ask you, Nuala O'Loan called for an independent commission of Dr. Haass, an historical investigations unit. In your view, in all of your views, is that—and that does not in any way preclude an independent inquiry of the Finucane case, but for these other cases, is that something that would yield results, in your opinion, Ms. Hall?

Ms. HALL. It was very interesting to see the dialogue today. Dr. Haass was very clear that he spoke basically on behalf of the parties.

Mr. SMITH. Right.

Ms. HALL. So was giving voice to people from Northern Ireland, Baroness O'Loan, from the United Kingdom.

What Amnesty International has said is that one mechanism that is comprehensive is absolutely essential. The people of Northern Ireland, with the various political parties and the Governments, the United Kingdom Government and the Irish Government, should make the decision about what that looks like. From Amnesty International's perspective, the requirement, the sole requirement would be that any mechanism must conform with the United Kingdom's international human rights obligations. It has to be independent, thorough, effective, impartial, and ensure that perpetrators are held accountable and victims have effective redress.

Mr. SMITH. Thank you. So the current mechanisms, just to be clear, are broken and need to be replaced with a mechanism that is all those things you just said?

Ms. HALL. Yes.

Mr. SMITH. Ms. Finucane brought up the whole issue of the restriction notices and you—just for the record, I and others did write the Members of Parliament when they were considering a terrorism law and the ability to convey to Ministers a veto power over what goes forward or not.

It seems to me that, again, this is another area where a coverup is not too strong of a word. Nuala O'Loan mentioned in her testimony, or testified about the gate-keeping function played by the legacy unit, which employs former Special Branch officers. It seems to me that such an independent inquiry would have to be able to overcome that obstacle as well, otherwise, under a false notion of national security, people who have committed atrocities will be concealed or hidden from any kind of accountability; is that correct?

Ms. HALL. There are two issues here: One is the independence, which of course former RUC Special Branch officers have no place investigating violations by RUC Special Branch, even if they occurred 20 or 30 years ago. So I think that in terms of independence, that is a critical issue.

The second point to make on the notion of, you know, what is required, we have not actually said whether it should be an actor from outside of Northern Ireland or whether it should be composed of people from Northern Ireland, but it is absolutely clear that in the North, very few people have been untouched by the conflict, and if you are not untouched, it means that you cannot be impartial. So our call would be to ensure that there is independence and impartiality as well as effectiveness and thoroughness.

Mr. SMITH. Mr. Devlin testified that the perpetrators have generally been rewarded with pensions, promotions and medals, there is a message in that. Ms. Hall, how would you respond to that, talking about the MRF?

Ms. HALL. You will note in our report that we do not reference the MRF, and I feel uncomfortable discussing a factual situation with which I have very little firsthand knowledge. But do let me say that it is not the first situation of post-conflict where we have seen the perpetrators of crimes, the perpetrators of violence actually go up the ladder.

Right? It is a way of rewarding people who essentially were seen at one point as helping to protect the state, but from Amnesty International's point of view, national security concerns can never trump fundamental human rights. Patrick Finucane's life was taken, Mr. Devlin's life was threatened. Those are crimes under international law, and the invocation of protecting the state or national security can never trump such fundamental human rights protections.

Mr. SMITH. Thank you.

Chairman Rohrabacher.

Mr. ROHRABACHER. Thank you very much, Mr. Chairman.

And, again, let me just say it is always an honor to be working with Chairman Smith. He is a man of great honor and integrity, but also a man of truly a commitment to humanity. And I have known—after my 25 years I have been here in Congress, and he is one of my most respected colleagues, in my eyes.

And I am trying to grasp what the best way to make a better world is here, and I know we have just—I think we need to make sure we have everything in perspective as well. We are talking about violence that took place against people who were not engaged in violent activity, were not engaged in terrorism, but violence that was conducted by authorities on people who were not engaged in violence.

But at that time, there were a lot of people engaged in violence in that society, and we did have a situation where pubs were being blown up and Margaret Thatcher, I understand, her—there was an attempt on her life, and several people in the building, they have lost their lives when a bomb went off in the building that she was in. There was violence being committed.

Now, let me ask all the way down the line, we are talking about justice for people who committed murders who were part of the other side, are we not? I mean, we want investigations not just of the officials that were engaged in this, but also perhaps people who were in the IRA at the time who planted bombs and killed numbers of civilians; is that right, Ms. Hall?

Ms. HALL. I am sorry, Chairman Rohrabacher, you were otherwise engaged with business and you stepped out.

I had mentioned in my comments that one of the key issues for Amnesty International is further investigation of the policies and practices of the armed groups, of all of the armed groups——

Mr. ROHRABACHER. All right.

Ms. HALL [continuing]. Including the IRA, so, yes——

Mr. ROHRABACHER. Thank you.

Ms. HALL [continuing]. In fact, abuses by all sides.

Mr. ROHRABACHER. Yeah. I have some constituents out, and one thing about democracy, we have to pay attention to our constituents, so I had a group of constituents I had to say hello to and focus on that for a few minutes.

Thank you for that answer. That is exactly the right answer. You know, there is—we know that in the past we have had leaders of countries who earlier on had committed acts of violence against civilians, do we not? And I think the one that everybody knows about is Mr. Begin, in Israel, who helped bomb the King David Hotel, where I happen to stay. And they make a big deal out of it in the King David Hotel, where they actually have a video of the bombing and then they have a video when Begin came back 20 years later as the Prime Minister to the hotel.

Tell me, would the approach that we are trying to take today, would that make peace any better, any easier if Mr. Begin would have been prosecuted instead of—which they did, they did not focus on that, but said 20 years later, he was elected to Parliament.

In fact, he became the Prime Minister; is that what we are talking about?

Ms. FINUCANE. I would say in our case, we have never sought prosecutions——

Mr. ROHRABACHER. All right.

Ms. FINUCANE [continuing]. Against those that perpetrated the crime against my husband, but what we—a statement I made many, many years ago was in Northern Ireland at the time my husband was shot, gunmen were two a penny. It wasn't hard to get somebody to pull a trigger. And I have never really been interested in the person who pulled the trigger. I am interested in the people behind that, who sent that man out.

Mr. ROHRABACHER. Uh-huh

Ms. FINUCANE. And I want to know how far up the chain of command that went.

Mr. ROHRABACHER. I think that that is very legitimate for someone, anyone who is—it is even legitimate for Mr. Devlin to say, who shot me and at least let's hold someone accountable, if nothing else, for an apology for maybe shooting someone that they——

Mr. DEVLIN. Well, sir, you had made a comment earlier on about giving it up and that in the past was the past and let bygones be bygones.

Mr. ROHRABACHER. Could you talk a little bit closer to the mike?

Mr. DEVLIN. I am sorry. You had made a point earlier on of letting the past be the past and letting bygones be bygones.

Mr. ROHRABACHER. Yes.

Mr. DEVLIN. The Israelis never let the past be the past and let bygones be bygones. To this day they still hunt down the people who carried out the Holocaust.

These people carried out a heinous crime in Northern Ireland, and something has to be done.

Mr. ROHRABACHER. I will say this, that my reading of this, and I am just not an apologist for Israel and anything they do is right, but——

Mr. DEVLIN. Right.

Mr. ROHRABACHER [continuing]. My reading is if there was an agreement with the Palestinians tomorrow, the Israelis would let bygones be bygones and actually live at peace with the people who are going to live at peace with them. It is the ongoing conflict that creates this hatred, and the idea is to try to stop——

Mr. DEVLIN. People just want——

Mr. ROHRABACHER [continuing]. To try to stop this type of violence.

Mr. DEVLIN. People just want the truth. They are not looking to have people hang them from a flag pole, they are looking to have the truth.

Mr. ROHRABACHER. Good.

Mr. DEVLIN. And if you can't give us the truth, then what are you hiding? The British Government are hiding stuff. The people that were in power at the time are hiding stuff. They have to come out and tell people what went on. It doesn't matter what you say, how you pinned it. These were criminals that carried these crimes out. We know they may not go to jail, but God Almighty, the people that gave them the orders to do it have to be brought to justice.

Mr. ROHRABACHER. Well, if you are calling for accountability and truth, you are pleading your case and people are—and myself and others are totally on your side on that call. I mean, this is obviously accountability, but accountability doesn't necessarily mean going back 20 or—one thing is locating people who were involved in conflict, it is another thing after 30 or 40 years.

When I said 25 years, it was 25 years since someone murdered your husband. 25 years. It was—but you are right, you are right. You deserve to know who was involved in that and you deserve to know if the British Government was involved in approving that, you deserve to know that, and the public deserves to know that, and that is how we will get people in government to make right decisions, knowing that eventually the truth will come out if they make a criminal decision like to kill an unarmed person or to terrorize a population. So that, I don't have any disagreement with that. Don't think because I am trying to figure out a way to get people to live in peace with one another.

I will say that there are still 50 pages of the Warren Commission report that have not been made public. And I am one of the—I don't know if are on this, Chris, but I am, I am one of the guys saying everything should be open after 50 years, for Pete's sake, the American people should know everything.

And, frankly, it shouldn't even be 50 years and it shouldn't be 25 years; at least as soon as possible is to get an honest assessment of situations like this, the public should know that. And Amnesty International's been playing a wonderful role in trying to expose these evils that governments have done around the world.

So again, I love Ireland. And I will have to say, I honestly believe that had Ireland not been split with those six counties in the north and, you would not have this problem today, because the Irish throughout the rest of that area are not—the Protestants and the Catholics are not at each other's throats in the Republic of Ireland.

And so it behooves us to make the right decision on these dramatic era issues of what is going to be one country and sovereignty, et cetera, rather than just trying to get over the hump. And what happened in—as we know in 1920 and at that time, the British people were just tired of fighting, what agreement can we make, and they just went ahead and agreed to a rotten agreement, and that is why we are still trying to solve it today. But, that is a whole other issue.

And, ma'am, I am sorry that your husband was taken away and shot. I mean, that is a horrible thing.

Ms. FINUCANE. It may seem like a distant time for you, and you keep referring back to things that happened in the past and maybe letting them go, but for me, it is a current issue, and in 25 years in practically every one of those 25 years, there has been new information come to light, so it is never an in-the-past issue, not for me or for other people in Northern Ireland.

Mr. ROHRABACHER. I understand.

Ms. FINUCANE. And although it started off as questions about the murder of one man, it has now come to be a collusion policy that was carried out against every single person in Northern Ireland. No matter who you were or what you did, if you were dispensable, you could be disposed of. And we want that exposed, we want the people who put that policy in place made accountable.

And you referred earlier on to picking at a little scab. I myself used an analogy for many years that what is happening in Northern Ireland, and not just in my case, is a deep, deep wound, and you cannot cover a deep wound up. If you stitch it up, it will fester and it will burst, and what you need to do is deal with it and pack it and start at the bottom, and then you end up with practically no scar at all, and that is what we need.

Because I do one case, because I fight for my husband's name, but it has come to mean quite a lot in Northern Ireland, and many people who are unable or unwilling to stand up and be as public as I am, encourage me to continue, because they know that if the truth comes out in my case, it will satisfy them. And that is all they want: Truth and justice.

Mr. ROHRABACHER. That was a very fine retort. Thank you.

Ms. FINUCANE. Thank you.

Mr. SMITH. Thank you very, Chairman Rohrabacher.

Just a couple final comments. You know, one of the things about the Finucane case that got me personally, but also our subcommittee, so focused, including resolutions that passed in the House overwhelmingly that I authored, was the denial, the lies, the multi-layered deception that was engaged in by the British Government. And only in recent vintage did they come forward and suggest that there was collusion, but had you, Geraldine, accepted those lies, not only would the case of your husband's mistreatment, the cruelty that was meted out against him and yourself and the family who witnessed this terrible murder, but it would have enabled those lies and that deception to have further credibility and credence going forward.

This is one big massive coverup that needs to be exposed, and I can assure you that this subcommittee and this chairman will not cease so long as I have breath to do so.

I also would ask of Mr. Devlin, in the Panorama documentary by the BBC, the three people who speak on record on camera were proud——

Mr. DEVLIN. Yeah.

Mr. SMITH [continuing]. Proud. You watch that, you see a pride come through this TV screen for the killings that they engaged in; no remorse, no sense of, we have done wrong, I beg your forgiveness.

If you could—when you watched that, and of course you were a part of that show, but when you watched it, what was your reaction looking at cold-blooded murderers talking about drive-by shootings and the like?

Mr. DEVLIN. At that time, it was just like a common thing in Northern Ireland, as Mrs. Finucane just said, that no one knew who was doing what, and there was—everybody was, like, colluding with someone.

The RUC were colluding with someone, the British Army were colluding with someone. They were all—it was like a big game to them. And if these guys were on TV, the way they talked, it was like they were going out for a cruise that night, and it was like a drive-by shooting that you would see in a gangland in LA or in South America, that is what they thought they were doing. They just thought this was okay: We don't have anybody to answer to, because we have been given carte blanche.

And they did that and they did it throughout the years. Right up until the peace process, they were still doing.

Mr. SMITH. As you watched the documentary, what was your reaction in watching?

Mr. DEVLIN. I just thought they were murderers and animals and they need to be—listen, I know they might not get any jail time, statute of limitations or whatever it is, but these people have to be put up on a dock and asked why did you do this and who did—told you to do this. But they were animals, they were just pure animals. They—they were like the Black and Tans reincarnated, only they were called the MRF.

Mr. SMITH. Would you like to add anything before we conclude the hearing, any of our witnesses?

You know, Geraldine, our first hearing on your husband, you will recall, was back in 1997. Michael testified at that. We will not give up until the public inquiry, full, independent with all facts on the table occurs and—and we will not give up as a committee, I can assure you, with good, strong support from both sides of the aisle, until that which is hidden becomes known.

I do plan on introducing a resolution. The gist of it will be focusing on the whole concept of an independent commission along the likes of Nuala O'Loan and what Special Envoy Haass, Ambassador Haass, talked about. As you pointed out, Ms. Hall, the current systems are not working.

I would suggest cynically that while they may have had a good beginning, many of the guts of it have made it designed to fail, and it is failing, so we will work.

I would invite your input as to what should go into that resolution. And I was just reminded, I did remember, Julia Hall testified at that 1997 hearing as well. So thank you for your long stay and your focus on this as well.

Ms. HALL. I did.

Mr. SMITH. Thank you.

The hearing is adjourned.

[Whereupon, at 4:47 p.m., the joint subcommittee was adjourned.]

A P P E N D I X

Material Submitted for the Record

JOINT SUBCOMMITTEE BRIEFING & HEARING NOTICE
COMMITTEE ON FOREIGN AFFAIRS
U.S. HOUSE OF REPRESENTATIVES
WASHINGTON, DC 20515-6128

Subcommittee on Africa, Global Health, Global Human Rights, and International Organizations
Christopher H. Smith (R-NJ), Chairman

Subcommittee on Europe, Eurasia, and Emerging Threats
Dana Rohrabacher (R-CA), Chairman

March 11, 2014

TO: MEMBERS OF THE COMMITTEE ON FOREIGN AFFAIRS

You are respectfully requested to attend an OPEN briefing and hearing of the Committee on Foreign Affairs, to be held jointly by the Subcommittee on Africa, Global Health, Global Human Rights, and International Organizations and the Subcommittee on Europe, Eurasia, and Emerging Threats in Room 2172 of the Rayburn House Office Building (and available live on the Committee website at www.foreignaffairs.house.gov):

DATE: Tuesday, March 11, 2014

TIME: 2:00 p.m.

SUBJECT: The Northern Ireland Peace Process Today: Attempting to Deal With the Past

BRIEFER: The Baroness Nuala O'Loan
                   (Former Police Ombudsman for Northern Ireland)
                   (Appearing via videoconference)

WITNESSES: Panel I
                   The Honorable Richard N. Haass
                   Chair
                   Panel of Parties in the Northern Ireland Executive

                   Panel II
                   Ms. Geraldine Finucane
                   Wife of slain human rights attorney Patrick Finucane

                   Mr. Eugene Devlin
                   Victim of the Military Reaction Force

                   Ms. Julia Hall
                   Expert on Criminal Justice and Counter-Terrorism in Europe
                   Amnesty International

By Direction of the Chairman

COMMITTEE ON FOREIGN AFFAIRS

MINUTES OF SUBCOMMITTEE ON _Africa, Global Health, Global Human Rights, and International Organizations_ HEARING

Day __Tuesday__ Date __March 11, 2014__ Room __2172 Rayburn HOB__

Starting Time __2:05 p.m.__ Ending Time __4:45 p.m.__

Recesses | __0__ | (____to ____) (____to ____) (____to ____) (____to ____) (____to ____) (____to ____)

Presiding Member(s)

Rep. Chris Smith

Check all of the following that apply:

Open Session ☑   Electronically Recorded (taped) ☑
Executive (closed) Session ☐   Stenographic Record ☑
Televised ☑

TITLE OF HEARING:

The Northern Ireland Peace Process Today: Attempting to Deal With the Past

SUBCOMMITTEE MEMBERS PRESENT:

AGHGHRIO: Rep. Randy Weber
EEE&T: Rep. Dana Rohrabacher, Rep. William Keating, Rep. George Holding

NON-SUBCOMMITTEE MEMBERS PRESENT: _(Mark with an * if they are not members of full committee.)_

HEARING WITNESSES: Same as meeting notice attached? Yes ☑ No ☐
(If "no", please list below and include title, agency, department, or organization.)

STATEMENTS FOR THE RECORD: _(List any statements submitted for the record.)_

Proposed Agreement Among the Parties of the Northern Ireland Executive, submitted for the record by Dr. Richard Haass
Statement from the Pat Finucane Center, submitted for the record by Rep. Chris Smith
Statement from Patricia Lundy, submitted for the record by Rep. Chris Smith
Amnesty International report: Northern Ireland: Time to Deal with the Past, submitted for the record by Ms. Julia Hall

TIME SCHEDULED TO RECONVENE _____
or
TIME ADJOURNED __4:45 p.m.__

Gregory B. Simpkins
Subcommittee Staff Director

MATERIAL SUBMITTED FOR THE RECORD BY THE HONORABLE RICHARD N. HAASS, CHAIR, PANEL OF PARTIES IN THE NORTHERN IRELAND EXECUTIVE

PROPOSED AGREEMENT
31 DECEMBER 2013

AN AGREEMENT AMONG THE PARTIES OF THE NORTHERN IRELAND EXECUTIVE

on

PARADES, SELECT COMMEMORATIONS, and RELATED PROTESTS; FLAGS AND EMBLEMS; and CONTENDING WITH THE PAST

PROPOSED AGREEMENT
31 DECEMBER 2013

Introduction

We in Northern Ireland have come a long way. From the depths of violence, we have built an impressive, albeit incomplete, peace. More than fifteen years have now passed since the Belfast/Good Friday Agreement. In those years Northern Ireland has reached several milestones, including the decommissioning of arms, the St. Andrews Agreement of 2006, and the Hillsborough Castle Agreement of 2010, which paved the way for policing and justice powers to be devolved. Political structures are in place and structures of cooperation are established. Power-sharing has encouraged and enabled individuals once at odds to work together as partners in governance.

Despite these positive steps, we have further distance to travel. Many continue to await the end of sectarianism and the peace dividend that should be all citizens' due. The division of our society runs through our schools and our neighbourhoods. Efforts envisaged as part of the outworkings of the peace process remain unfinished and 'parity of esteem' remains a work in progress. Despite the admirable efforts of individuals and organisations across the public and non-governmental sectors, many in our society struggle with needs stemming from decades of conflict. These trends jeopardise both the progress we have made to date and our ability to extend it into the future.

The past year has been particularly challenging. We have witnessed friction and civil disorder. We have also seen continued acts of violence committed by those who wish to thwart Northern Ireland's progress toward a shared and peaceful future.

Last spring saw the publication of the 'Together: Building a United Community' strategy by the Office of the First Minister and deputy First Minister (OFMDFM). This was the latest in a series of efforts, including 'A Shared Future,' published under direct rule in 2005, and a public consultation on the Programme for Cohesion, Sharing, and Integration of 2010. This Agreement Among the Parties of the Northern Ireland Executive stems from the work of a panel established pursuant to 'Together: Building a United Community.' As this document stated:

> We recognise that there remain difficult and contentious issues in our society. In order to take forward work on these issues, we will establish an All Party Group which will have an independent Chair from outside the political parties. The All Party Group will consider and make recommendations on matters including parades and protests; flags, symbols, emblems and related matters; and the Past. The Group will report to the First Minister and deputy First Minister. The Group will establish mechanisms to hear from the various stakeholders across our community as to how best to address these difficult and contentious issues.

PROPOSED AGREEMENT
31 DECEMBER 2013

In accordance with this, the Panel of Parties in the Northern Ireland Executive was constituted under a chair, Richard Haass, and a vice chair, Meghan O'Sullivan. The panel included two members from each of the five parties in the Executive, with the addition of the two Junior Ministers.

The Chair and Vice Chair prioritised from the start engagement with civic society and the public. They established a website with a public submissions channel that attracted over six hundred submissions. During several visits to Northern Ireland, the Chair and Vice Chair held more than one hundred meetings with a broad range of groups, panel members, and officials from across Northern Ireland. Panel members, too, conducted their own intensive outreach and engagement in connection with their work on the panel.

It was in this context that the members of the Panel of Parties in the Northern Ireland Executive conducted the negotiations leading to this agreement. We carried out this work in support of the vision, expressed in 'Together: Building a United Community,' of a future based on equality before the law, equality of opportunity, good relations, and reconciliation. Our discussions have been designed to bring forward a set of recommendations that will provide long-term, sustainable solutions that are in the best interests of the society and that will make the peace more resilient. This agreement is part of our commitment to contending with the legacy of the past and to creating a modern, compassionate society. We firmly believe that the steps outlined here will help build a more united community where the needs of those who have suffered as a result of violence are addressed; where everyone has the ability to peacefully celebrate his or her culture; where the rule of law is upheld; and where public space is shared, open, and accessible to all.

Although we believe this agreement constitutes a significant step forward, it does not resolve all difficulties around the issues addressed. We could not reach an accord on initiatives to manage the issue of flags and emblems. Moreover, while we agreed a number of steps to contend with the past, other steps proved beyond consensus. This document is a contribution to addressing these difficult issues, not a solution.

Just as the construction of this agreement required consultation with a variety of stakeholders, it will require the work of many to implement. It is not self-enacting, even though it represents a consensus among the five parties. We will do our part and are committed to working with others to give effect to what is agreed here.

We are standing at a crossroads in Northern Ireland. This is a remarkable opportunity to make bold choices to address the issues that hold us back from meeting our society's full potential. Further delay will risk an increase in levels of public disengagement. The passage of time—and the passing of those with information to

PROPOSED AGREEMENT
31 DECEMBER 2013

share and wounds to salve—will also deprive Northern Ireland of the chance to learn as much as possible about its history while there is still time to do so. This loss would compound the social and emotional costs of our prolonged conflict.

We recognise that many of the initiatives outlined in this agreement will demand a substantial investment of financial and other resources. At a time of continuing economic challenges, some may wonder why attention should be given to these issues, potentially at the expense of others. But we believe the measures we have agreed to here constitute important investments in Northern Ireland's future. Progress on the issues we face would reduce the costs of policing our society and promote tourism, investment, commerce, and other durable economic gains.

We recognise that the issues we are addressing are in many ways reflections as much as causes of our society's challenges. Difficulties surrounding parades and protests, flags and emblems, and the past are symptoms of much deeper divisions. But those problems could well be far less daunting, far lighter a weight, were we able to face them with this agreement as a backdrop. As this work goes forward, rigorous equality of opportunity and equality before the law, mutual respect, and application of the rule of law must be the governing principles for Northern Ireland, not just now but permanently.

The complete version of this document can be accessed at:
http://www.northernireland.gov.uk/haass.pdf

MATERIAL SUBMITTED FOR THE RECORD BY THE HONORABLE CHRISTOPHER H. SMITH, A REPRESENTATIVE IN CONGRESS FROM THE STATE OF NEW JERSEY, AND CHAIRMAN, SUBCOMMITTEE ON AFRICA, GLOBAL HEALTH, GLOBAL HUMAN RIGHTS, AND INTERNATIONAL ORGANIZATIONS

SUBMISSION FOR THE RECORD TO CONGRESSMAN CHRIS SMITH, CHAIR OF THE HUMAN RIGHTS SUBCOMMITTEE

FROM: Anne Cadwallader and Alan Brecknell of the Pat Finucane Centre, MARCH 2014

The Pat Finucane Centre (PFC) works to uphold human rights and for equality of treatment under the law in Northern Ireland, believing that a past failure to do so was the single most important cause of the conflict that has blighted so many lives for 35 years.

We are named after the Belfast attorney, Pat Finucane, whose work in the same area was seen as threatening by those in the police and military establishment who were then disregarding the rule of law – leading to his murder at their hands.

Other campaign groups in Northern Ireland rightly focus on human rights abuses by paramilitary groups, both loyalist and republican. The PFC's main focus is on abuses carried out by the state, believing it has a duty under international treaties and conventions to uphold the highest human rights standards.

This is not our singular focus, however, and we offer assistance to anyone who asks for our help irrespective of their political or religious background, without charge and in total confidence.

Believing that this work is important for both principled and practical reasons, the PFC has been engaged in research to uncover the truth behind collusion for the last fifteen years.

We believe individual families bereaved by collusion between the state and loyalist paramilitaries certainly deserve truth and justice. We also believe that both our society as a whole would benefit immensely from honestly facing up to the wrongs that were inflicted on both communities by the state.

This important work had small beginnings in 2000 when Alan Brecknell, now one of our six staffers, sought the Centre's help to find the truth on whether his father, Trevor, had been murdered by state forces as he had heard.

Having discovered this was true, and that Trevor's murder was inextricably linked to others, Alan and the Centre began researching other murders in the same area around the same time.

This work included:

+ Analysing declassified state documents in the Irish and British national archives
+ Working with both statutory and informal sources on both sides of the border
+ Liaising with other human rights NGOs in Britain and the Republic of Ireland
+ Engaging with the Police Ombudsman, the Barron Inquiries ordered by the Irish government and with the Historical Enquiries Team (a unit within the Police Service of Northern Ireland).

Gradually, the Centre uncovered disturbing facts about a killer-gang comprised of both loyalist paramilitaries and state forces who killed over 120 people between 1972 and 1976.

We emphasise here that our work is focussed only on the facts as we establish them. The word "collusion" has sometimes been abused for propaganda purposes. We do not believe this serves families bereaved in the conflict – or wider society - any purpose.

We worked closely with families throughout this process, keeping them fully informed every step of the way and taking our guide from their wishes and priorities. Collectively, we kept our findings confidential until we had firmly established as many facts as possible.

The culmination of this work came in October 2013 with the publication of "Lethal Allies: British Collusion in Ireland" by Mercier Press of Cork, Ireland.

It tells how the most primary human right of all - the right to life – was disregarded by those whose task it was to uphold the law. The book names most of those responsible, details the murders on a case-by-case basis, includes in-depth interviews with the families, and lays bare the patterns of British government policy behind these tragic events.

The book has been reprinted five times; topped the Irish best-seller lists and has been discussed at the House of Commons, London, at Dáil Éireann and at the European Parliament in Brussels, Belgium.

Our full findings are included within the book's 416 pages. The findings are fully sourced and remain unchallenged either in detail or in whole by the Police Service of Northern Ireland; the Northern Ireland Policing Board; the British government (including the Ministry of Defence) or any other authoritative state or non-state institution or grouping.

Our findings include:

+ That members of the Royal Ulster Constabulary worked alongside loyalist paramilitaries in attacking Catholic civilians (source: the HET report on an attack on The Rock Bar).

+ That paid agents of the RUC within loyalist paramilitary groups were murdering Catholic civilians with impunity (source: the HET report on the Miami Showband massacre).

+ That the RUC Special Branch was refusing to share intelligence with those investigating these murders (source: the HET report on The Step Inn bombing)

+ That senior officers, at the highest level within the RUC, were corruptly refusing to take disciplinary action against colluding fellow officers even when provided with evidence of collusion between agents and Special Branch (sources: the HET reports on the Miami Showband Massacre, The Rock Bar and The Step Inn)

+ That members of the Ulster Defence Regiment (the UDR – the locally-recruited and largest regiment in the British Army) did the same – ie colluded with loyalist paramilitaries in murder

+ That the subversion of the UDR by loyalist paramilitaries was well-known from as long ago as 1972 and was tolerated and even encouraged by senior security personnel at the Ministry of Defence in London (see National Archive UK declassified documents on file with the PFC and referenced in "Lethal Allies")

+ Little or nothing was done to prevent this subversion which continued until the UDR's final disbandment (some would argue it continues to this day)

+ That it was well-known and established that weapons were being routinely stolen by loyalist subversives within the UDR and used to murder Catholic civilians – yet nothing was done to investigate or prevent the thefts

+ That loyalists were using their weapons training to murder Catholic civilians.

These conclusions bring disgrace, not only to the individuals responsible, but onto the British government of the time. They require an urgent response and, ultimately, acknowledgement, apology and reparations to the families so grievously bereaved.

Currently, over 25 families have cases before the Northern Ireland Policing Ombudsman. The families are also on the brink of civil legal action in the Northern Ireland courts while renewed inquests into many of these cases are also pending.

Taking the wider view, people and politicians from outside Northern Ireland often wring their hands and ask why, twenty years after the IRA and loyalist ceasefires, the "two communities" remain bitterly divided.

As recently as last week, US President Bill Clinton said it was time to "finish the job" of peacemaking reflecting continuing concerns over issues such as the legacy of the past (as well as conflicts over parading and the use of perceived sectarian flags in public places).

The PFC believes that stabilising a permanent peace through reconciliation in Northern Ireland would be far easier, and become far more likely if our shared past is examined, openly and honestly.

US politicians have paid a key role in the Northern Ireland peace process and are again having a positive effect now with the publication of the proposals made by Dr. Richard Haass and Professor Meghan O'Sullivan.

The part of these proposals addressing the past are, we consider, an acceptable compromise that could pave a way forward (subject to provisos allowing, for example, the addressing of concerns of families of victims killed outside Northern Ireland including those killed in Britain, the Republic of Ireland and elsewhere).

The Haass/O'Sullivan proposals are the best, and possibly only, chance to provide bereaved families with the truth about their relatives' deaths and to offer hope of healing society's wounds by an honest investigation of the conflict.

Their success or failure currently hangs in the balance as the two main unionist parties reject their implementation.

Meanwhile, the PFC's book, "Lethal Allies", shows what positive outcomes are possible, given an independent truth-recovery process.

This past, as the PFC's recent research and analysis of official documents reveals, includes the issue of systemic collusion between elements in both the police and military with loyalist paramilitary groups.

We believe that this collusion was fostered as part of official British government policy, honed in various previous colonial conflicts including insurgencies in Kenya, in Malaya, Aden and Cyprus.

It was as a crude and illegal tactic, both domestically and internationally, in Britain's counterinsurgency armoury but – far from preserving life – it fomented the conflict and fuelled the flames of violence.

Although the main objection to collusion is principled and based on legal norms, it can be seen empirically that Catholic confidence in the rule of law collapsed, leading to greater support for republican paramilitary groups.

As support for them burgeoned, leading to greater violence, members of the two main locally-based governmental security institutions also suffered as the IRA attacked both on and off-duty members of the RUC and UDR.

We hope and believe that our work culminating in "Lethal Allies: British Collusion in Ireland" has the potential to change the narrative of the conflict in Ireland from that of "two warring tribes".

We appeal to US politicians to assist us in our work and to bring whatever influence they have on those who currently do not see the Haass/O'Sullivan proposals as the way forward.

Time is short. The parents of some victims have already died. Others are aged and ill. Any further delay compounds the injustices already inflicted on the bereaved.

Justice delayed is justice denied and, although many families realise that justice is now beyond their grasp, they at least deserve an honest attempt to establish the truth.

WRITTEN SUBMISSION OF PROFESSOR PATRICIA LUNDY, UNIVERSITY OF ULSTER TO THE JOINT SUBCOMMITTEE BRIEFING & HEARING COMMITTEE ON FOREIGN AFFAIRS:

"THE NORTHERN IRELAND PEACE PROCESS TODAY: ATTEMPTING TO DEAL WITH THE PAST"

Background

In any dialogue on how to deal with the legacy of the past in Northern Ireland it is important to assess the current mechanisms and to what extent they are 'up to the task'. Since 2005 I have carried out independent in-depth research and analysis of the Police Service of Northern Ireland's Historical Enquiries Team (PSNI/HET). In March 2012 I presented testimony to the Foreign Affairs Committee ("Prerequisites for Progress in Northern Ireland" hearing) on recent research findings.[1] The research specifically considered HET's review processes and procedures in Royal Military Police (RMP) investigation cases involving the fatal shooting of over 150 citizens by the British army between 1970 and September 1973; including the activities of the Military Reaction Force (MRF) a secret military terror unit reported to be involved in at least ten of these deaths.[2] I highlighted anomalies and inconsistencies in the HET investigation process where the military was involved, compared to historic cases where non-State or paramilitary groups were implicated. I suggested there was a differentiation in treatment and that State-involvement cases were treated more favourably and were investigated with less rigour.[3] I questioned whether such anomalies and inconsistencies impacted upon the ability, and or perception, of the HET to undertake impartial, effective Article 2 compliant reviews in cases involving State agencies.

The research was also presented to the Human Rights and Professional Standards Committee of the Northern Ireland Policing Board (NIPB) (8 March 2012). At the time the research was dismissed by the Chief Constable. The NI Policing Board (NIPB) put further questions in respect of the research to the PSNI at a meeting held on the 5 April 2012. This led directly to the Minister of Justice, at the request of the Chief Constable, commissioning an investigation into the work of the HET by Her Majesty's Inspectorate of Constabulary (HMIC). In July 2013 HMIC published a damming report on the HET. The NI Policing Board issued a press release stating it had **no confidence in the leadership of the HET**.[4] All HET military case reviews were suspended and they remain 'on hold'. The Chief Constable offered a personal apology to Professor Lundy.[5]

---

[1] See Lundy, Patricia *(2012) Research Brief: Assessment of the Historical Enquiries Team (HET) Review Processes and Procedures in Royal Military Police (RMP) Investigation Cases download at* http://eprints.ulster.ac.uk/21809/

[2] BBC One- Panorama: Britain's Secret Terror Force http://www.bbc.co.uk/programmes/b03jprmx; BBC News - Undercover soldiers 'killed unarmed civilians in Belfast' http://www.bbc.co.uk/news/uk-24987465

[3] In 2005 the Historical Enquiries Team (HET) was set up as a specialist unit of the Police Service of Northern Ireland (PSNI) to examine over 3,000 conflict-related deaths in Northern Ireland between 1968 and the Good Friday Agreement in 1998.

[4] BBC News, "NI Policing Board declares 'no confidence' in HET" see, http://www.bbc.co.uk/news/uk-northern-ireland-23181060; and NI Policing Board http://www.nipolicingboard.org.uk/news/article.htm?id=14330

[5] Steve Otter of HMIC publicly stated, "What is indefensible is that she [Pro Lundy] did make these findings in 2009, so for four years nothing was being done to address those findings and I do find that that is very difficult to believe. See, BBC News, "HET Treat State Cases with Less Rigour" http://www.bbc.co.uk/news/uk-northern-

In this written submission I wish to update the Committee on progress with regard to RMP cases and the implications for any assessment of attempts to deal with the past in Northern Ireland.

Current Mechanisms: The 'Package of Measure'

The UK government was found in breach of Article 2, the right to life, in a number of cases in Northern Ireland. In a joint judgment delivered on 4 May 2001 the European Court of Human Rights (ECtHR) set out the elements which must be adhered to for an investigation to be Article 2 compliant — effectiveness, independence, promptness, accessibility to the family and sufficient public scrutiny.[6] In response to the above judgments, the UK Government presented the ECtHR with a "package of measures", which it claimed were necessary steps to address the issues raised in the Court's judgment and would ensure future Article 2 compliant investigations. The key institutions in the package of measures are the Police Ombudsman's Office, the Historical Enquiries Team (HET), the coroner's courts, and public inquiries.[7] It is important to note that the Committee of Ministers, the body responsible for the implantation of ECtHR judgments, considered the HET could play an important role "when taken together with other measure"[8] designed to satisfy the State's obligation to conduct effective investigations in alleged violations of Articles 2 of the ECHR. Over a decade later numerous authoritative commentators have concluded that the package of measure is deficient and incapable of dealing with Northern Ireland's legacy issues. In short, there are significant delays, deficiencies and obstruction of the implementation of ECtHR judgments. In July 2013 the European Court found that the inquest system was 'structurally incapable' of holding Article 2 compliant inquests. The Police Ombudsman's Office was recently the focus of three separate critical investigations and reports[9] which found, amongst other things, 'a lowering of operational independence'. The Ombudsman Al Hutchison took early retirement. The Office has recently been the subject of reform and is under new leadership. However public confidence was shaken in this important element of the package of measures. The former Police Ombudsman publicly acknowledged that the current number of historic cases referred by HET will take his office 50+ years to complete; more cases are likely to follow.

---

ireland-23161353. There have been ongoing questions raised by the NIPB why for over four years the PSNI did nothing to address the research findings first published by Prof Lundy in 2009.

[6] Which encompasses the cases *Jordan v UK* (No. 24746/94); *McKerr v UK* (No.28883/95); *Kelly and Others v UK* (No.30054/96); *Shanaghan v UK* (No.377715/97).

[7] The 'package' (a combination of new and pre-existing elements) includes deploying the Police Ombudsman's Office (OPONI) to conduct historic investigations in complaints against the police, 'calling in' other police forces to investigate deaths, establishing the Serious Crime Review Team (now Historical Enquiries Team (HET)), facilitating judicial review by families of decisions not to prosecute, introducing new practices relating to verdicts of coroners' juries and to disclosure at inquests, and other measures following reviews of the coroners' system, developing Initiatives in relation to legal aid, establishing a number of Inquiries into alleged state involvement in contentious deaths; and the enactment of the Inquiries Act 2005.

[8] CM/Inf/DH(2008)2 revised 19 November 2008 – HET is **part** of a process and package of measures.

[9] Tony McCusker, Department of Justice, June 2011; Michael Maguire, Criminal Justice Inspectorate, June 2011; Committee on the Administration of Justice, June 2011.

The HET: Research Findings and Assessment

The following is a summary of my research findings on the HET. The HET is promoted by the PSNI and Northern Ireland Office (NIO) as an effective mechanism capable of meeting victims' needs and delivering its objectives. The research provides empirical evidence which qualifies and/or challenges official claims of efficiency and whether objectives have been met. The research found differentiation in treatment and deficiencies in PSNI/HET investigations. It exposed anomalies and inconsistencies in the investigation process where State agencies were involved compared to non-state or paramilitary suspects. It found a differentiation in treatment in State-involvement cases; less robust investigations and more favourable treatment in cases involving the British army, compared to killings involving non-State actors.[10] If HET processes are incapable of holding perpetrators to account, or if there is failure to follow obvious lines of enquiry, this is unlikely to satisfy Article 2. Recent changes in PSNI structures mean HET no longer has responsibility for investigations where historic reviews identify evidential, arrest and prosecution opportunities. These cases are now transferred and are under the control of C2 Department of the Police Service of Northern Ireland (PSNI). It is worth noting that <u>no RMP investigation was transferred from HET to C2/PSNI</u> in cases where there were new evidential opportunities but many non-state cases had been referred for formal investigation. The research raised serious questions about the ability of the HET to undertake independent, impartial, effective investigations in cases involving State agencies and/or that may touch upon the police themselves; and whether it was Article-2 compliant and UK government obligations deriving from ECtHR judgements were being met.

In addition, the research found that there was lack of independence relating to the role of intelligence gatekeepers and the influence of 'corporate or institutional memory' through rehiring of retired police officers.[11] The lack of independence with regards to the HET's Intelligence Unit alone goes to the heart of whether HET is Article 2 compliant. Every stage of HET's work was found to be compromised by lack of independence. The research also found that access to the 'truth' was delimited by HET procedures and victims had to know the 'right questions' to ask. The quality and depth of reports improved significantly when NGOs, legal or other representatives assisted victims' families. The Unionist community, and bereaved families of the British army, were shown to be less well represented. This lack of representation influenced the quality of their HET reports and access to justice. In contrast to official claims, interviews with victims revealed dissatisfaction with HET output and a failure to answer some families' questions. However, other families have expressed satisfaction with the HET process and their reports. Some families do not seek investigations and/or prosecutions. However, accountability processes for historic crimes cannot be put to one-side or relinquished at the request of victims' families.

Importantly, the serious defects described above could have implications for the viability of the package of measures; that is, HET could <u>undermine the entire package of measures.</u>

---

[10] For a full discussion see, Lundy, P (2012) *Assessment of HET Review Processes and Procedures in Royal Military Police (RMP) Investigation Cases* download at http://eprints.ulster.ac.uk/21809/.

[11] For a detailed discussion of these concerns see, Lundy, Patricia (2009) *Can the Past Be Policed? Lessons From the Historical Enquiries Team Northern Ireland, Law and Social Challenges, Vol. 11. pp. 109-171* download at http://eprints.ulster.ac.uk/2459/

Her Majesty's Inspectorate of Constabulary's (HMIC) Inspection of HET

HMIC's Review was conducted between November 2012 and May 2013 and the inspection report published July 3rd 2013 was highly critical of HET. [12] The inspection focused on whether the HET's approach to reviewing military cases conforms to current policing standards and policy; if it adopts a consistent approach to all cases (i.e. both military and paramilitary cases); and if the HET's review process meets the requirements that would ensure it is compliant with Article 2 of the European Convention on Human Rights and Fundamental Freedoms (i.e. independence, effectiveness, promptness, and transparency and accountability). It is not possible to discuss all HMIC findings. The following is a brief summary.

HMIC inspection found that:

> ➢ The HET is not conforming to current policing standards in a significant number of important areas. In particular, HMIC found a lack of explicit systems and processes; different teams adopting different working practices; no clearly defined complaints process; and no independent review of the HET's processes;
> ➢ The HET treats state involvement cases differently <u>as a matter of policy</u> and this appears to be based on a misinterpretation of the law. This is entirely wrong, and has led to state involvement cases being reviewed with less rigour in some areas than non-state cases;
> ➢ HET had "acted outside the law";
> ➢ HMIC noted practices such as how interviews under caution were conducted, the nature and extent of pre-interview disclosure, and the process by which claims made by state agents about suspects being unfit for interview under caution were not verified. These practices undermined HET's capability to fully determine if the state's use of force was justified in some investigations.
> ➢ That many of these findings had been made by Prof Lundy in her first report submitted to NIPB in November 2008 and for four years nothing was done to address those findings.
> ➢ As a result, HMIC considers that the HET's approach to state involvement cases is inconsistent with the UK's obligations under Article 2 ECHR.

The Current Position: Northern Ireland Policing Board, Working Group on HET

As a consequence of HMIC's critical report, and as mentioned above, the NIPB issued a press release which stated it had no confidence in the leadership of the HET. The NIPB set up a Working Group to oversee HMIC's recommendations. The Working Group has held consultation meetings with a range of stakeholders between July and February 2014 and its recommendations are pending. I am firmly of the view that HMIC's recommendations did not go far enough. HET is irretrievable and a completely new independent mechanism is required. I agree with other commentators that HET cannot be made Article 2 compliant; it

---

[12] Inspection of the Police Service of Northern Ireland Historical Enquiries Team, HMIC 2013 http://www.hmic.gov.uk/media/inspection-of-the-police-service-of-northern-ireland-historical-enquiries-team-20130703.pdf

will not meet the required benchmarks.[13] To 'patch it up' with even further PSNI involvement will <u>not</u> restore trust and confidence in this highly damaged process. HMIC recommended an Oversight Panel as a means to monitor the work of the HET. I doubt whether a panel, even if made up of five or six respected individuals, employed on a full time basis, with unfettered access, could satisfactorily retrieve the situation. Families and NGOs have lost faith in the process. This is the crux of the matter. A range of victims groups and human rights NGOs have unanimously and publicly stated that they 'would not recommend any family to engage with HET'.

Attempting to Deal with the Past: 'Haass Talks Proposals'

In Northern Ireland, the policy approach to dealing with the past has been fragmented and highly contested. The alternative model takes as its starting point the 'transitional justice' mechanisms employed in other transitional societies, and seeks to tailor such solutions to Northern Ireland. An alternative model received some powerful support when in 2009, the former UK government-appointed Consultative Group on the Past (CGP), led by Lord Eames and Denis Bradley, issued a report recommending the establishment of a Legacy Commission for Northern Ireland, largely along international truth commission lines. The core proposal was the establishment of an independent Legacy Commission that would create processes of reconciliation, justice and information recovery. It was envisaged that there would be review and investigation of historical cases; a process of information recovery; and examination of linked or thematic cases emerging from the conflict. These proposals drew on extensive consultations across Northern Ireland.

The 'Haass All Party Talks' proposals appear to build on the CGP recommendations and provide a very promising blueprint to establish a mechanism that can deal comprehensively with the past in Northern Ireland. The Haass proposals for a Historical Investigations Unit (HIU), with the full investigative powers of the Police Service of Northern Ireland (PSNI), to take over the cases now being addressed by the Historical Enquiries Team (HET) and the historical unit of the Police Ombudsman of Northern Ireland (PONI); and an Independent Commission for Information Retrieval (ICIR) to enable victims and survivors to seek and privately receive information about conflict-related events, would be a significant improvement on what is currently on offer. There is now considerable empirical evidence that the 'package of measures' is not working and incapable of adequately dealing with the past in Northern Ireland.

Patricia Lundy
Professor of Sociology
University of Ulster
Northern Ireland

---

[13] "Even with significant reform CAJ does not believe it is possible for the HET to meet the necessary requirements of independence and impartiality in relation to state involvement cases"; see, S420 CAJ's submission to the Northern Ireland Policing Board Working Group on the PSNI, Historical Enquiries Team (HET), http://www.caj.org.uk/contents/1202

INTRODUCTION

"It's said they are waiting for us to die out. But the next generation will still keep asking questions about what happened. Look at me, it was my grandfather who was killed and I am still going to keep asking for the truth."

James Miller, whose grandfather David Miller was killed in a suspected IRA bomb attack in Claudy, County Londonderry/Derry, on 31 July 1972. Eight other people were killed and 30 people were injured. Interview with Amnesty International, 5 February 2013.

"From my family's point of view all we want to know is the truth. We would like a truth-seeking mechanism where people have to speak about what they were involved in, where there can finally be full acknowledgment of the things that were done here."

Alan Brecknell, whose father Trevor Brecknell was killed on 19 December 1975 in a gun and bomb attack on Donnelly's Bar, Silverbridge, County Armagh, attributed to the UVF. Patrick Joseph Donnelly and Michael Francis Donnelly were also killed and six people were seriously injured. Interview with Amnesty International, 20 February 2013.

Decades after their relatives were killed, many families from across communities in Northern Ireland still ask how and why a family member fell victim to a deadly attack in one of post-war Europe's most intense periods of political violence. Fifteen years after the signing of the Belfast/Good Friday Agreement, they – together with many victims of torture, ill-treatment, abductions and other human rights violations and abuses – are still waiting for truth, justice and reparation.

This report focuses on the search for truth in Northern Ireland. Truth is an essential element of the duty to investigate human rights violations and abuses, of a victim's right to remedy, including reparation, and in combating impunity. It can help victims, families and communities understand what happened to them, allow those responsible to be identified, counter misinformation and misconceptions about the past, and allow lessons to be learnt to ensure that abuses are not repeated. This, in turn, may contribute towards the process of reconciliation between divided communities. Denial and silence increase mistrust and damage the social fabric, exacerbating existing divisions.

Obstacles to laying bare the truth have come in many forms in Northern Ireland. Since the negotiation of the Belfast/Good Friday Agreement, the UK government has failed to make dealing with the past a priority – in part, one suspects, because human rights violations by state actors would also come under scrutiny. Some former protagonists, their advocates and their associates, who have transitioned to peaceful, electoral politics, also appear to see little to gain from confronting the abuses that were committed by all sides – including, of course, their own. Politicians in Northern Ireland have so far failed conspicuously to come together and agree how to effectively address the legacy of the past. However, despite the political reluctance, many victims and their families yearn for a true account of the violations and abuses committed against them and consider it a prerequisite for moving forward with their lives and ensuring a lasting peace.

The signing of the Belfast/Good Friday Agreement on 10 April 1998 signalled a turning point in the history of Northern Ireland. In the 30 years preceding the 1998 Agreement, Northern Ireland had experienced a period of intense political violence, which left over 3,600 people dead and over 40,000 others injured.[1] Human rights violations by state actors and abuses by armed groups were perpetrated by all sides, in many cases with impunity, leaving a devastating impact – felt to this day – on the population.[2]

Fifteen years on, remarkable progress has been made in moving towards a more peaceful future for Northern Ireland. Indeed, Northern Ireland is often presented as a success story and, in many respects, it is. However, this prevailing narrative of "success" has also been used by politicians – in both Belfast and London – to obscure and ignore the need to confront the legacy of the past and the demands of victims and their families.

Though several mechanisms do exist to examine various violations and abuses committed over three decades of political violence, their work has not been consistent or comprehensive. The narrow and specific remits of these mechanisms have resulted in a patchwork and piecemeal "system" of investigation in Northern Ireland that is not capable of delivering the full truth about the human rights violations and abuses that took place.

The international human rights framework stresses the importance of ensuring justice, truth and reparation in response to violations and abuses. Governments, including the UK, have a duty to investigate killings, suspicious deaths, life-threatening attacks, torture and other ill-treatment, and bring those responsible to justice in a fair trial. The authorities must ensure that victims have access to processes that allow them to find out the truth of what happened and victims must be provided with full and effective reparation to address the harm they have suffered and help them rebuild their lives. This is important in particular for communities emerging from protracted periods of violence and seeking to achieve sustainable peace.

The first part of the report provides an overview of the 30 years of political violence and charts some of the changes following the 1998 Agreement. This cannot and does not offer a comprehensive account of Northern Ireland's history and all the changes that have occurred with peace; rather it provides the context for the report. The report goes on to set out the UK's obligations to investigate human rights violations and abuses and ensure that victims have access to the truth and receive full and effective reparation to address the harm they have suffered. It argues for the importance of such measures, both to individuals and to society as a whole, particularly as Northern Ireland continues to face violence and division.

The second part of the report considers the work of the mechanisms to which victims and families have turned in order to try to establish the truth and secure justice and reparation. It assesses these mechanisms against relevant international human rights law and standards.

No single mechanism has been established in Northern Ireland with the mandate to examine the past systematically and comprehensively. Instead several separate, distinct mechanisms have been established or directed to investigate past violations and abuses. These mechanisms are:

◼ the Historical Enquiries Team (HET), which is part of the Police Service of Northern Ireland and reviews deaths arising from the violence;

◼ the Office of the Police Ombudsman for Northern Ireland (OPONI), an independent body that is able to investigate historical allegations of misconduct by the police;

▢   coroners' inquests, which have powers to establish who the deceased person was, when, where and how they died;

▢   public inquiries, which have been established in a small number of cases;

▢   the Police Service of Northern Ireland (PSNI), which carries out criminal investigations into historical cases, often as a result of evidence having been uncovered by one of the preceding mechanisms.

Although some of these mechanisms have the potential to work well – and some have done so in specific instances – by and large they either have fallen or are falling short of human rights standards because of their failure to conduct prompt, thorough and effective investigations in an independent and impartial manner. This has undermined confidence and trust in their ability to deliver the truth about the past.

Even if all these mechanisms worked perfectly, Amnesty International would remain of the view that the piecemeal approach to investigations adopted in Northern Ireland is too diffuse and too incomplete to provide a comprehensive picture of all the violations and abuses that occurred during the decades of political violence. Inherent limitations within the mechanisms, and their discrete, individualized nature, have meant that much of the truth remains hidden while those in positions of responsibility have remained shielded. It has also contributed to a failure to develop a shared public understanding and recognition of the abuses committed by all sides.

In the light of these shortcomings, the third part of the report, highlights the need for investigations that will effectively examine:

▢   all human rights violations and abuses, including those resulting in serious injury and cases of torture and other ill-treatment carried out by both state and non-state actors;

▢   patterns of abuse by armed groups and violations by the state and the examination of systemic issues that arise;

▢   the role and actions of particular state institutions such as the prosecution authorities, the civil service, and the government during the conflict, as well as the knowledge and responsibility of those in high-level positions of authority;

▢   state policy or state-sanctioned practices and whether they deliberately or indirectly gave rise to unlawful conduct; as well as the institutional culture of the security forces or other governmental apparatus or agencies and whether it fostered the perpetration of human rights violations and abuses and a climate of impunity;

▢   the degree and level of collusion between the state and armed groups;

▢   the institutional culture of the armed groups, their policies and practises, and the knowledge of and responsibility for human rights abuses of those in high-level positions of authority in those groups.

The fourth and final part of the report sets out the case for establishing a single comprehensive mechanism to deal with the past in Northern Ireland. Such a mechanism should provide victims and society as a whole with the truth to the fullest extent possible about violations and abuses and contribute to ensuring justice and reparation. It should be victim-focused and be able to, among other things, investigate all outstanding cases and patterns of abuses and violations, have powers to compel witnesses and documents and be able to develop recommendations aimed at securing full reparation for victims and helping to bring an end to violence and division. Drawing on Amnesty International's past experience and research across the globe, the report outlines central principles to help guide the establishment of such a mechanism.

The lack of political will to address the past remains the greatest obstacle to establishing a single comprehensive mechanism in Northern Ireland. Without the truth, however, Northern Ireland's past will continue to cast a long, damaging shadow over its present and its future. The longer that truth is kept hidden, and as a result justice and reparation are denied, the greater the potential for damage. The longer each bereaved family or injured individual is left to stitch together facts and fragments of information from disparate, piecemeal processes, the greater their pain.

Amnesty International therefore calls on all political leaders to garner the will and courage to establish a single overarching mechanism capable of comprehensively addressing the past, ensuring that a future can be built that is genuinely shared and sustainable.

METHODOLOGY

Amnesty International has carried out research across the three decades of violent political conflict in Northern Ireland and documented a range of human rights violations and abuses, including unlawful killings, torture and other ill-treatment, abductions and unfair trials.[3] A key part of the organization's work has been to campaign for effective investigations and for victims to be able to secure their right to remedy and reparation. This report draws from that research and builds on the organization's calls for truth, justice and reparation.

This report uses the term "conflict" in its ordinary and general sense, not as a legal term. As used in this report, the term "conflict" is not intended to convey the legal meaning that the term "armed conflict" has in international humanitarian law.

The three decades of violence had an impact beyond Northern Ireland, with attacks in other parts of the United Kingdom, the Republic of Ireland and Europe. This report, however, focuses on the mechanisms that currently exist in Northern Ireland for the investigation of historical cases. It is based on research conducted by Amnesty International during six visits to Northern Ireland between March 2012 and July 2013. During these visits Amnesty International delegates conducted a total of 47 detailed interviews with relatives of people who died in conflict-related killings in Northern Ireland. Some of those interviews were conducted individually and some in groups. Of these cases 17 incidents were attributed to republican armed groups, resulting in 68 deaths; 23 to loyalist armed groups resulting in 40 deaths, including some cases of collusion; and six incidents that resulted in 26 deaths were attributed directly to the security forces (including the Royal Ulster Constabulary (RUC), as the police force at the time was known, and the British Army).

Amnesty International sought out victims and families from different communities and conducted interviews across Northern Ireland, including in Armagh, Ballymena, Ballymoney, Belfast, Claudy, Downpatrick, Dungannon, Enniskillen, Londonderry/Derry, Lurgan, Magherafelt, and Omagh. Amnesty International also met with people from different communities who were seriously injured during the decades of political violence.

In some instances, individuals asked not to be identified by name, in order to protect their privacy or, in some

The complete version of this document can be accessed at:
http://www.amnesty.org.uk/sites/default/files/time_to_deal_with_the_past_0.pdf

Amnesty International September 2013   Index: EUR 45/004/2013

www.ingramcontent.com/pod-product-compliance
Lightning Source LLC
Chambersburg PA
CBHW080317290526
45790CB00005B/2075